Enriching the Lives of Children

Enriching the Lives of Children: Creating Meaningful and Novel Stimulus Experiences to Promote Cognitive, Moral and Emotional Development

By

Rosalyn M. King

Cambridge Scholars Publishing

Enriching the Lives of Children: Creating Meaningful and Novel Stimulus Experiences to Promote Cognitive, Moral and Emotional Development, by Rosalyn M. King

This book first published 2008 by

Cambridge Scholars Publishing

15 Angerton Gardens, Newcastle, NE5 2JA, UK

British Library Cataloguing in Publication Data
A catalogue record for this book is available from the British Library

Copyright © 2008 by Rosalyn M. King

All rights for this book reserved. No part of this book may be reproduced, stored in a retrieval system, or transmitted, in any form or by any means, electronic, mechanical, photocopying, recording or otherwise, without the prior permission of the copyright owner.

ISBN (10): 1-84718-442-1, ISBN (13): 9781847184429

TABLE OF CONTENTS

List of Illustrations vii
Acknowledgements viii
Abstract ix

Part One:
Introduction 1
Historical Reflections
The Meaning of Enrichment
Why Should We Worry About Enriching Children's Lives?

Part Two:
Theoretical Propositions in Support of Enriching Children's Lives 7
Constructivism, Authentic Pedagogy, Learning and Assessment
Learning, Meaning and Understanding

Part Three:
Learning and the Developmental Domains 14
Learning and Cognitive Development
Connecting Developmentally Appropriate Practices to Brain Research
Development of Moral Character
Stimulating Emotional Development
Creativity and Development

Part Four:
Structures and Strategies for Creating Novel Stimulus Experiences 40
Educating the Whole Child
Teaching for Multiple Intelligences
Guided Discovery
The Importance of Play
The Concept of Flow
Differentiated Instruction
Role of Technology
Impact of Computer-Based Technologies
Innovative and Futuristic Technologies

Part Five:
Selected Innovative Models 69
Overview
Tables 5.1 through 5.9

Conclusions 107
Key Findings
Gaps in the Research

Notes 114
References 115
Appendices 129

List of Illustrations

Figures

3.1   12 Point Comprehensive Approach to Character Education 27

Tables

1.1   Education's Ideological Divide 4
3.1   Overview of Developmentally Appropriate Practices and Connections Between Recent Findings on Brain Research 20
3.2   Sternberg's 21 Ways to Encourage Creativity in Children 35
4.1   Overview of Multiple Intelligences from Howard Gardner 45
4.2   Multiple Intelligences Menus 46
4.3   Characteristics of Mature Play 50
4.4   Impact of Technology on Children's Social, Emotional, Language, Physical, Motor and Cognitive Development 56
4.5   Impact of Technology on Four Characteristics of Learning 61
4.6   Summary of Select Disciplines Using Computer-Based Technology 64
5.1   Overview of Select Innovative Programs, Models and Strategies by Category 71
5.2   Selected Large-Scale Programs 74
5.3   Selected Innovative Teaching Strategies 82
5.4   Teaching for Multiple Intelligences—Models and Programs 88
5.5   Inquiry and Problem-Based Models 92
5.6   Science Models 94
5.7   Service and Field-Based Models 95
5.8   Innovative Instructional Technology Models 97
5.9   Projects with a Global Focus 103

ACKNOWLEDGEMENTS

This book began as a presentation at the Oxford Roundtable on the Psychology of the Child at St. Anne's College, Oxford University. Support and participation was made possible through a grant from the *NVCC Educational Foundation, Inc.,* and the *King Family Trust Fund.*

Acknowledgement also is given to my parents, the late *Morris C. King, Sr.,* and *Marie King Koon;* my dearest late aunt, *Mable King Martin* and my late grandmother, *Rosa L. King*. These members of my family were some of the most influential teachers who shaped my early and later life; and, were instrumental in filling my life with enriching experiences. I am truly blessed because of their love and sacrifices. I am deeply appreciative.

Rosalyn M. King

ABSTRACT

This book is a theoretical discussion on enriching the lives of children. It examines the research on promoting and enhancing cognitive, moral and emotional development in children. It is a state of the art assessment of the theories, explanations and strategies proposed or implemented relative to the topic and research findings.

Distinctions are made between the traditional descriptions of enrichment versus constructivists' notions about enrichment. Discussion also includes other cognitive and cognitive developmental theorists' explanations and models, along with suggested methodologies for educationally and personally enriching and stimulating the lives of children. The research principally investigates the use of authentic and innovative pedagogy and practice as a way of making meaningful and holistic connections to enliven children's learning.

Discussion includes the historical backdrop of the study, theoretical propositions in support of enriching children's lives, learning and the developmental domains, including a discussion of cognitive, social, emotional, and moral development; and the relationship between creativity and development. Further, an examination is made of the research literature to find interesting structures and strategies for creating novel stimulus experiences for children, and includes a discussion of potentially impactful concepts.

Finally, an overview of selected program models assessed by this researcher as innovative, novel or workable in their approach and application toward stimulating children's educational and personal development are presented and discussed. These models are also presented in a typological framework.

PART ONE

INTRODUCTION

This book explores ways to maximize the lives of children and to enhance their growth and development by advocating for the provision of meaningful, novel, stimulating, and enriching experiences as part of the teaching and learning process. The ultimate goal of these strategies should be to promote cognitive, moral, and emotional development in student learners. I am particularly interested in exploring the types of enrichment experiences currently in existence or proposed in the research literature that would have the above stated end results in children.

Over the decades, there have been two main streams of philosophy and practice permeating education—traditionalist mainstream notions about education and those who advocate for more alternative or innovative approaches to mainstream strategies. Likewise, relative to enrichment programs for children, one can find the more traditional approaches being used to provide support to development of the basic skills of reading, writing, math, verbal abilities, and so on. There are also the traditional enrichment programs around subject matter content such as math and science particular career development enrichment programs. For many of us, these more traditional approaches to education have been the norm. However, many educators would say that these notions are no longer as effective as perhaps they were in the past. They would argue that today's educational systems include a different breed of students with differing and varied interests, abilities, and attention spans; and, many of these students are more global in scope and perspective based on societal, national and world interests, areas of focus and overall growth and development of the nation and world. What becomes imperative to investigate is how the current paradigm might change to reflect the transitions and challenges we confront in the 21st century, with the changing face and perspectives of students worldwide. Questions to be pondered are some of the following:

- What reforms have been made and what further reforms are needed since the call for educational reforms in the 1970s?

- How can we create classrooms that are exciting and stimulating places for students to be?
- Is there a possibility that the traditional modes and the alternative innovative modes can meet?
- How do we transition from the more traditional modes of teaching to dynamic models of teaching and learning that truly stimulate and motivate student learning?
- Over the past two decades, who has developed or implemented innovative theories, explanations, or model programs addressing the importance of enriching the lives of children and targeting developmental domains?
- What key elements are being espoused as important?
- What are the interesting and novel models being implemented and tested?
- Are model programs having successful results?
- Is there conclusive evidence as to the effectiveness of programs being developed; and, are they designed to enrich the lives of children in meaningful and positive ways? What specific developmental domains are addressed?
- What are the gaps in understanding, research and types of programs needed?

This is the challenge of education in every decade, in every century. A response to these and other questions is the major impetus for this exploration. Further, this researcher would like to know the true nature of the state of affairs relative to educational programs designed to enrich the lives of children. Moreover, it would be helpful to provide a synthesis of those providing futuristic thinking and developing new and innovative approaches and proposals about teaching and learning toward these ends. The current call for reforms in education are advocating for teaching for understanding, meaning, connection to the student and a holistic approach to educating children, adolescents and others.

Historical Reflections

In the middle to latter 1970s, educator, John Goodlad, reported that schools and classrooms were some of the most boring places for students to be (1977). Goodlad spent thousands of hours studying schools and classrooms and began calling for reforms. In addition, more than twenty years ago, the National Commission on Excellence in Education (1983), developed a report entitled *A Nation at Risk* and called for reforms in education. The Commission indicated that American education faced a rising tide of mediocrity unless actions were taken to raise expectations and achievement. In reviewing education initiatives over the past decades, many believe this goal has yet to be realized. Diane Ravitch, educational historian and research professor, indicates the changes wrought by twenty years of task forces, committees, and study groups have not produced the hoped-for improvement in student achievement; and, few of the Commission's recommendations were properly implemented and did not bring about effective educational reform (2003). She reveals that a new report from the Koret Task Force on K-12 Education at the Hoover Institution concludes that it is now time to go beyond the recommendations set forth by the National Commission in 1983. This new task force is calling for a reinvigorated reform agenda for schools, with the choice of bringing flexibility and innovation as to how education is provided. Further, they call for a transparency to reveal information about how the education system is working; and, accountability to demonstrate that children are learning. According to Ravitch, the real issue remaining is whether schools will be "good enough" to prepare students for the challenges of the 21st century.

Some believe we can have the best of both worlds—traditionalism and innovation and one researcher coined the term "innovative traditionalism" (See Ferrero 2006). Yet, others believe that even with failing reforms the United States remains the superpower, dominating the world, and is the most scientifically and technologically advanced nation. Further, they believe that perhaps the reforms were trying to fix a problem that really was not broken (Zhao 2006). Zhao believes that the reform initiatives neglected to focus on providing students with a curriculum that focuses on international issues that actively engages them in global affairs and provide a lack of opportunities for impoverished children to participate in current and future globalization discourse.

Table 1.1 presents an overview of education's ideological divide as described by Ferrero (2006).

TABLE 1.1 Education's ideological divide

TRADITIONAL	INNOVATIVE
Standardized Tests	Authentic Assessment
Basic Skills	Higher-Order Thinking
Ability Grouping	Heterogeneous Grouping
Essays/Research Papers	Hands-on Projects
Subject-Matter Disciplines	Interdisciplinary Integration
Chronology/History	Thematic Integration
Breadth	Depth
Academic Mastery	Cultivation of Individual Talents
Euro centrism	Multiculturalism
Canonical Curriculum	Inclusive Curriculum
Top-down Curriculum	Teacher Autonomy/Creativity
Required Content	Student Interest

Source: Ferrero 2006.

The Meaning of Enrichment

Even though we freely use the word "enrichment" and call many of our educational programs "enrichment programs," in-school, after-school or Saturday academies, no formal definition could be found of the concept. The word, "enrich" has been described in some of the following ways: *"to add greater value or significance to;" "to improve in quality or productivity* (as by adding desirable ingredients);" *"to supply with riches or wealth"* (Random House Webster's College Dictionary); *"to make rich or richer"* (The New Merriam-Webster Dictionary); *"to improve the quality or value of;" "to make wealthy or wealthier"* (Compact Oxford English Dictionary).

For the purposes of this paper, *enrichment* is defined as:

> "Improving the quality and value of one's life through nurturance and development of one's human potential by provision of stimulating experiences that energize the individual to act in positive and productive ways; and, with the end result being enhanced growth and development that leads to a higher quality of life, greater productivity, balance and wholeness."

The beneficial outcome of such enrichment should result in riches and wealth, both personally and materially.

Why Should We Worry About Enriching Children's Lives?

Children are the future leaders of the world, if it is to survive. Exploring more effective ways to enhance human growth and development in novel ways is imperative, if we are to prompt them to learn, grow, develop, reflect, apply, and act. Parker Palmer (1999) advocates that it is the purpose of education to guide students on an inner journey toward more truthful ways of seeing and being in the world. David Perkins (2004) indicates that the purpose of education is not just about acquiring knowledge, but about learning how to do significant things with what you know. Howard Gardner would agree as he indicates that a good measure of intelligence is a student's ability to fashion products. The constructivist theorists would argue that students must be permitted the freedom to think, to question, to reflect, and to interact with ideas, objects, and others—to construct meaning (Brooks and Brooks 1999).

Moreover, we know that the current traditional modes of education are not working for many – and that the traditional modes of assessment fall short of the mark. Also, there is an increasing number of students who are classified as having some type of learning disability, such as attention deficit disorder or attention deficit hyperactivity disorder among other labels. It is difficult to keep the new breed of students focused on subject or task in the traditional teaching modes. Therefore, the existing paradigm presents a challenge and anomaly. The time is ripe for a scientific and educational transformation that leads to a new framework to meet the needs of the new breed of students, shaped by the circumstances, events, values and norms of the current society, nationally and globally.

Historically, the Academy has come a long way in our understanding about what is necessary to provide for the nurturance of children. This is true when you review the history of child development and notions about the purposes of children-from abuse as infants to using them in child labor in factories to allowing them to hang on the streets before the creation of kindergarten, to calling them "little savages." Understanding of the importance and need for children's nurturance and development, including the education of parents and teaching professionals have been important steps in making progress toward creating enriching experiences for children.

The call to enrich the lives of children is the call to give the children of the world every opportunity to evolve into psychologically healthy, whole, viable, and productive human beings who will contribute to the good of self, society and world; and which will hopefully lead to a richer and better world in which to thrive and grow. Developing pedagogy and strategies that permit more collaboration, a drawing out of the unique talents, interests, and creative aspects of individual children is imperative.

PART TWO

THEORETICAL PROPOSITIONS IN SUPPORT OF ENRICHING CHILDREN'S LIVES

This section investigates the extent to which the research literature supports this author's claim that creating novel enriching experiences for children is important to their growth and development. What follows is a description of the theoretical propositions or concepts offered in support of the importance of finding novel ways to stimulate and enrich children's learning and their lives.

Constructivism, Authentic Pedagogy, Learning and Assessment

The 1980s reportedly ushered in new interpretations about learning from the old notion that learners were treated as "disconnected knowledge-processing agents," to a newer notion that learners are "active knowledge-makers or constructors" who bring to their learning a wide range of social and cultural experiences (Bloomer 2001). But as reported by Bloomer, the notion of constructivism is not new, it has actually been around for quite a long time, perhaps forgotten or overlooked by many. The idea that learning entails the creation of knowledge from experience can be traced back at least as far as Aristotle and to Kant (1704-1804) who claimed that knowledge was not 'human proof' but governed by the perceptual frameworks or schemata of the knower. Bloomer states that the idea that individuals construct unique understandings of their world is also a basic tenet of much of interpretive sociology, social philosophy and anthropology. For example, he cites the following:

"The phenomenologist, Husserl (1859-1938) argued that while knowledge is grounded in the 'lebenswelt' (life-world) and is to some extent shared; it is also the product of subjective experience. Weber (1864-1920), too, stressed the subjective basis of personal knowledge, claiming that action can only be properly understood if reference is made to the subjective meanings (personal constructions) maintained by the actor concerned. The work of Berger and Luckmann (*The Social Construction of Reality* 1967) also drew heavily from this phenomenological tradition."

Further, personal constructions or meanings are the conceptual tools of symbolic interactionism, the process by which meanings are conveyed, interpreted and acted upon. Individuals are likened unto actors, each seeking to impose their own definitions of the situation through presentation of self, but having to be responsive to other actors doing likewise. Thus, individual knowledge is constructed, contested, shared and changed. Many of these ideas, according to Bloomer, have been incorporated into more recent approaches to the study of learning. Constructivism, which has found favor particularly among mathematics and science educators, is prominent among these. Constructivism is described in many varieties and forms: trivial, radical, social and cognitive.

As cited by Bloomer (2001) in his work, early notions of constructivism are based on the premise that 'knowledge is not passively received but actively built up by the cognizing subject' (as cited in von Glasersfeld 1989, 182). Cognitive constructivism is based on the work of Piaget and focuses on the development of the cognitive schemes which make knowledge construction possible. It is concerned with the progressive adaptation of an individual's cognitive schemes to the physical environment (as cited in Driver, et al. 1994, 6) although some argue that schemata are not readily adaptable (as cited in Chinn & Brewer 1993). It is based on a highly individualistic model of human development and applied largely to the questions of pedagogy and teaching and, as such offers only limited opportunities for exploring connectivity.

Social constructivism—the social construction of meaning and personal knowledge in a symbolic world—draws from the work of Lev Vygotsky (1989-1934), although it is indicated that it also draws from the basic organizing ideas of phenomenology and symbolic interactionism (Bloomer 2001). Further, John Dewey's philosophy emphasized a constructivist approach when he indicated that children learn best when interacting in a rich environment, constructing learning from real life applications while using various senses simultaneously; and, as a result, the probability of learning is greater (Dewey 1964). The core of the concept of discovery and guided discovery learning also comes from Dewey's tenets.

Current constructivist theorists and other cognitive developmental theorists call for more authentic learning and assessment. Constructivist theorists' believe that learning is a constructive process in which the learner builds an internal representation of knowledge and a personal interpretation of experience. They believe that learning is an active process in which meaning is developed based on the experiences encountered. Learning is not linear. It does not occur on a time line of basic skills, but instead occurs at a very uneven pace and proceeds in many different directions at once. Further, constructivists believe that real-world contexts are needed if learning is to be constructed and transferred beyond the classroom (Brooks & Brooks 1999). Thus, according to these researchers, constructivism is a theory of learning that describes the central role that learners' ever-transforming mental schemes play in their cognitive growth and development. Therefore, learning has to be understood and internalized.

Howard Gardner's view of a constructivist classroom is that students are continually trying out ideas and practices to determine where their ideas work and where they prove inadequate. According to Gardner, the models an individual constructs in his or her mind are crucial to understanding (Scherer 1999). Therefore, learning, like life, is experiential and experimental. One must test notions and theories to determine whether they work.

According to theorists, there are 5 basic tenets of constructivism: 1) learning results from exploration, and discovery and meaning is constructed and reconstructed; 2) learning is a community activity facilitated by shared inquiry, including collaboration and cooperative inquiry; 3) learning occurs during the constructivist process where students learn concepts while exploring their application and learning through discovery; 4) learning results from participation in authentic activities, such as problems that students might encounter in the "real world;" and 5) outcomes of constructivist activities are unique and varied in that learners create knowledge from new information based on their previous experiences; thus, the results of projects will differ (Alesandrini & Larson 2002). Constructivists believe that it is important to help students find their own way by presenting them with the larger context of situations. This is similar to the gestalt's' belief that having a conceptual framework or holistic view of something is vitally important to understanding the component parts. It is believed that when educators design instructional practices to help students construct knowledge, then students learn.

Brooks and Brooks (1999) provide an accurate summary of the constructivist model:

> "Students must be permitted the freedom to think, to question, to reflect, and to interact with ideas, objects, and others—in other words, to construct meaning. In school, being wrong has always carried negative consequences for students. Sadly, in this climate of increasing accountability, being

wrong carries even more severe consequences. But being wrong is often the first step on the path to greater understanding." (24)

Fred Newmann and associates provide a slightly different view of authentic pedagogy as including three components: construction of knowledge, disciplined inquiry, and value beyond school. The construction of knowledge would challenge students to produce their own meaning and understanding rather than reproduce what one has been taught. Disciplined inquiry ask students to use a prior knowledge base from one or more areas or fields (facts, vocabularies, concepts, theories, algorithms, conventions), to seek in-depth understanding rather than a superficial awareness, and to express their conclusions through elaborated communication. In-depth understanding requires more than knowing lots of details about a topic. It occurs when students look for, test and create relationships among pieces of knowledge that can illuminate a given problem or issue. Relative to elaborated communication, Newmann and associates cite as end-result examples, the professional careers of scientists, jurists, artists, journalists, designers, engineers and other accomplished adults who rely on complex forms of communication, both to conduct their work and to express their conclusions. These professionals use verbal, symbolic, and visual language that includes qualifications, nuances, elaborations, details, and analogues, woven into extended expositions, narratives, explanations, justifications, and dialogue, to convey and communicate their work. In contrast, much of the communication required in current schooling requires only brief answers such as true or false, multiple choice, fill in the blank, or short sentences (Newmann et al. 1996). Moreover, a most important distinction between authentic intellectual achievement and conventional school achievement is that authentic achievement has value beyond school—*"aesthetic, utilitarian, or personal value apart from documenting the competence of the learner"* (284). These researchers indicate that when adults write letters, news articles, insurance claims, or poems; speak a foreign language; develop blueprints; create a painting or a piece of music; or build a stereo cabinet; these individuals attempt to communicate their ideas, produce a product, or have an impact on others beyond simply demonstrating that they are competent. Achievements of these sorts have special value. According to Newmann and associates, such achievements are missing in tasks contrived only for the purpose of assessing knowledge (e.g., spelling quizzes, laboratory exercises, or typical essay exams).

Therefore, according to Newmann and associates, learning is a complex active mental process. It is not achieved by merely transmitting information to a student, who has to reproduce what has been transmitted.

The student must work on processes, interpret and negotiate the meaning of the information encountered for learning to take place. This learning process is influenced by the student's prior knowledge; the social context of values, expectations and rewards; the sanctions in which information is initially communicated and later expressed by the student; and the student's self-monitoring in the process of learning. Newmann et al., summarizes their definition of authentic learning and achievement and indicates the slight difference from original constructivist notions.

> "Our emphasis on the construction of knowledge is consistent, with the constructivist perspective of the student as a meaning-making person continuously integrating prior experience with new information, even in the most traditional classrooms. But our vision extends this descriptive claim. We suggest that authentic intellectual achievement requires "construction" to reach beyond retrieval and imitation of knowledge previously produced by the self or others. Authentic construction of knowledge involves application, manipulation, interpretation, or analysis of prior knowledge to solve a problem that cannot be solved simply by routine retrieval or reproduction." (286)

Learning, Meaning and Understanding

How is learning connected to meaning and understanding? And, what does it mean to teach for meaning and understanding? A summary of the research over the last 30 years on learning and cognition reveals that learning for meaning leads to greater retention and use of information and ideas (Bransford, Brown & Cocking 2000).

In the early 1990s, Howard Gardner provided evidence from the findings of 30 years of cognitive research revealing that students did not understand much of what was taught to them. He indicated that students lacked the capacity to take knowledge learned in one setting and apply it appropriately in a different setting. He cites examples from observations of this fact. In addition, he found study after study that revealed that students lacked the capacity to take knowledge learned in one setting and apply it appropriately in a different setting. Further, all of the studies indicated that even the best students in the best schools could not apply what they had learned (Brandt 1993). This is similar to the findings of Max Wertheimer decades ago, in his work on productive thinking, where he found that students could not solve mathematical problems in novel ways when asked to think outside of the box from which they had been taught.

Many of the proponents would say that the search for meaning is the purpose of learning; so the teaching of meaning is the purpose of teaching (Brooks 2004). Education should have as its goal meaning making at the core of pedagogy and practice according to some. Teaching for the sole purpose of performing for the test, for many, defeats the mission of teaching for learning, meaning and understanding. Teaching for meaning requires the teacher to become a mediator of thinking through engagement of the student for understanding and learning. It is reported in the research literature that teachers who teach for meaning also make time for wonder—which means not rushing through materials and lessons to get to the next one, but really helping students understand subject matter and content. For example, one teacher states:

> "I want my students to look at a tree and think of the leaf patterns and the golden ratio, how chlorophyll changes with the seasons, how trees fit in the ecosystem. Our job is to get students to love learning and wonder why and how things work."(Brooks 2004,13)

According to some educators, teaching for meaning is an engaging idea, but many teachers find it problematic in this age of mandates and standardized tests (McTighe, Seif and Wiggins 2004).

Students can only find and make meaning when they are asked to inquire, think at high levels, and solve problems. According to research, teaching for meaning and understanding embodies five key principles:

- *Understanding big ideas in content;*
- *When students are asked to inquire, think at high levels and solve problems;*
- *When students are expected to apply knowledge and skills in meaningful tasks within authentic contexts;*
- *When teachers regularly use thought-provoking, engaging, and interactive instructional strategies.*
- *When students have the opportunity to revise their assignments using clear examples of successful work, known criteria, and timely feedback.*

(McTighe, Seif, & Wiggins 2004, 27)

Gardner believes that children must be provided with "multiple entry points" because children do not all learn in the same way; they do not find the same things interesting. And, based on the theory of multiple intelligence, one can approach any topic in a rich variety of ways. He states further: *"We need to give kids a chance in school to enter the room by different windows, so to speak but to be able to see the relationships among the different types of windows."* (6)

Gardner also indicates that schools should reduce its importance on coverage of material.

> "The greatest enemy of understanding is coverage." As long as you are determined to cover everything you actually ensure that most kids are not going to understand. You've got to take enough time to get kids deeply involved in something so they can think about it in lots of different ways and apply it—not just at school but at home and on the street and so on." (7)

Gardner believes that children do not understand mass chunks of information or that they forget information as soon as the test is over, because it has not been built or ingrained into their brain through the process of teaching for understanding.

PART THREE

LEARNING AND THE DEVELOPMENTAL DOMAINS

Learning and Cognitive Development

According to the literature, learning is a central part of children's lives and their development, but the study of learning shifted for a period and became only a rather peripheral part of the field of cognitive development (see Siegler 2000). The focus was more on cognition (thinking). Now educators are beginning to realize the interconnectedness between learning and cognition and would say that any theory of development that has little to say about how children learn is a seriously limited theory of development.

It is indicated that learning probably is even more central in the lives of children than in the lives of adults. In contrast, childhood is a period of life in which learning plays a particularly large role relative to performance. Infants, toddlers, and preschoolers frequently need to acquire new capabilities and their ability to learn is very important (Siegler 2000).

It is reported that the importance of children's learning for a coherent understanding of development has led a growing but small group of investigators to study learning as a critical part of development. Specifically, they investigate how children learn meaningful concepts and skills such as object permanence, reaching, face recognition, scientific and mathematical problem solving, arithmetic, and so on. Thus, the new field of children's learning, unlike the old one, emphasizes acquisition of concepts and skills that are important in children's lives (Siegler 2000).

Rogoff (1998) believes that within the sociocultural approaches to development, learning involves the incorporation of values and cultural assumptions that underlie views about how material should be taught and how the task of learning should be approached, rather than solely focusing on increasing knowledge of content. Other theories and models also attempt to explain children's learning, including the overlapping waves theory by Siegler (1996), which states that children typically use a variety of strategies and ways of thinking, rather than a single one to solve a problem; that these diverse strategies remain over time; and, that experience brings changes in relative reliance on existing strategies and ways of thinking, as well as the introduction of more advanced approaches.

Other models of children's learning, such as those constructed within dynamic systems theories differ in their particulars but share with overlapping waves theory a number of assumptions about how children learn. Within both, children learn by doing and learning occurs through performance (Siegler 2000). Another shared assumption is that a wide variety of constraints—anatomical, physiological, environmental, and cognitive—guide learning. It is believed that increasing the focus on children's learning will yield a more comprehensive understanding of development; it also may yield valuable educational applications.

The research literature indicates that it is no secret that many children do not learn well in school. Rigorous developmental analyses of how children learn—and fail to learn—may produce a better understanding of the learning difficulties and contribute to development of better strategies and programs.

Moreover, in light of the discussion on the relationship between learning and development, an interesting and relevant description of learning is offered by Renshaw who defines learning not as acquisition but as *"activity contributing to change and enrichment of the individual"* (1992). Therefore, it can be concluded that the purpose of learning is to enrich the lives of children, to take them where they are at their many ability levels and stimulate their growth and development in positive ways that would increase their developmental domains.

Connecting Developmentally Appropriate Practices to Brain Research

The National Association of the Education of Young Children (NAEYC) has recently adopted the constructivist approach to early childhood education. They provide an outline of the connections between their principles of developmentally appropriate practices (DAP), new research on brain development and learning, and suggested strategies for the classroom environment (Rushton and Larkin 2001). Their original developmentally appropriate practices had a philosophical orientation that advocated for didactic, teacher-centered approach to learning that encompassed primarily whole group instructional techniques. Now, the guidelines have been revised to describe a philosophical orientation that implies a constructivist approach to teaching young children. The guidelines are based on the premise that children are social learners who actively construct meaning and knowledge as they interact with their environment (Rushton and Larkin 2001).

Research on what constitutes appropriate early learning experiences has focused on both the social-emotional and cognitive domains of development during the past decade (such findings are cited in: Burts, Hart, Charlesworth & Kirk 1990; Hyson, Hirsh-Pasek, & Rescorla 1990; Dunn, Beach, & Kontos 1994; Sherman & Mueller 1996). Studies also indicate that children actively engaged in learner-centered environments score higher on measures of creativity, have better receptive verbal skills and are more confident in their cognitive abilities (Hyson et al. 1990; Dunn et al.1994). In addition, other evidence cited indicates that children who attended developmentally appropriate programs in preschool performed better in first grade on standardized assessments of achievement (Frede & Barnett 1992). Further, a study by Burts et al. (1993) indicated that children from low socioeconomic home environments who were enrolled in DAP kindergarten classrooms showed higher reading scores in first grade than their counterparts who attended more traditional classrooms.

Moreover, recent brain research also led to the revision of the guidelines on early childhood learning environments and developmentally appropriate practices (DAP). Brain research also supports the importance of developing and implementing a curriculum appropriate for the learner's developmental age.

Table 3.1 outlines the revised DAP principles as correlated with brain research findings and the suggested strategies for creating an ideal classroom learning environment. Some of the highlights of the discussion and rationale indicate the following:

- Learning does not take place as separate and isolated events in the brain—specific regions work together. For example, the temporal lobe relates to language development, writing, hearing, sensory association and memory. The parietal lobe relates to higher sensory abilities, language, and short-term memory. The frontal lobe aids us in our ability to judge, to be creative, make decisions and plan. Therefore, when a child is engaged in a learning experience a number of areas of the brain are simultaneously activated.
- Learning and memory are strongly connected to emotions, and therefore, the learning environment needs to be both stimulating and safe.

- Classroom experiences can be designed to allow children to investigate, reflect, and express ideas in a variety of ways that are increasingly complex and interconnected.
- Learners need ample opportunities to use and expand their preferred intelligences, as well as adapt to and develop the other intelligences, which are all interdependent within the one brain. Then they need opportunities to express what they know and understand in a variety of formats.
- Multiage grouping is one strategy that helps to facilitate learning for a range of abilities.
- Each child's uniqueness is expressed in a number of ways: personality, temperament, learning style, maturation, speed of mastering a skill, level of enjoyment of a particular subject, attention and memory. These attributes help to identify how a particular child will learn and what style of teaching is best suited for him or her.
- Each brain's growth is largely dictated by genetic timing, and is as individualized as DNA.
- There are no homogeneous groups of children; as no two children are the same, no two brains are the same. The environment affects how genes work and genes determine how the environment is interpreted.
- Providing hands-on activities that both cater to the differences among children and stimulate various regions of the brain reinforces stronger associations of meaning and makes learning inherently more interesting.
- Teachers who are trained to observe each child's development can establish a responsive environment for different documented stages of play (solitary, parallel, associative), and carefully design appropriate activities for the child's level. Teachers of older students can pay attention to higher order thinking skills in a similar manner, challenging students with engaging problem-solving opportunities.
- The teaching of complex skills too soon may impede learning, and conversely, not teaching children when they are ready may result in boredom and a lack of interest.
- Because each learner is different, children should be able to choose activities that fit their level of development, experience and interest. Thus, teachers will want to use a variety of teaching methods and materials to ensure that every child becomes interested in exploring ideas, to ensure their auditory, visual, tactile or emotional preferences are accounted for.

- Different children feel challenged by different problems, and threatened by different social circumstances, and this matters in what and how they learn.
- Each learning experience lays the groundwork for future learning, either positively or negatively. The child's ability to learn and interpret new information is directly related to the frequency of prior experience with related ideas.
- Brain research also indicates that certain windows of opportunities for learning exist. For example, the research literature cites animal studies where vision was obscured at key times in their development and these animals were unable to ever see again. A similar finding is the result for oral language.
- Language and motor development both require children to actively engage with others. Conversation and physical activity are extremely important for the development of the brain. Young children require opportunities to interact with each other regularly, encounter new vocabulary, construct arguments, express emotions, and stretch their muscles.
- Learning environments should encourage verbal interactions, moving around the room as children work on projects or pursue a line of inquiry, and plentiful occasions to use manipulative materials including gross motor equipment.
- Second language acquisition is most successful prior to fifth or sixth grade when the necessary structures in the brain for language learning are still in place. Introducing young children to more than one language is extremely beneficial, even if they do not yet understand how language is structured grammatically or written down.
- Since no two children learn at the same rate, it is crucial that children be given repeated opportunities and ample time to explore, play, and socialize while they work in various curriculum areas.
- Information is better presented in a context of real life experiences where new information can build upon prior knowledge, so that learners understand how it is meaningful to them.
- Field trips are an excellent example of a teaching strategy to connect new learning to real world applications. For example, when studying pollution, students might visit the landfill, clean water treatment center, recycling plant, local municipal garbage collection center rather than just viewing pictures or reading about the subject.
- The environment in which a child learns, both the explicit physical surroundings (people, manipulative materials, books) and the

implicit cultural norms (alphabet, numerical symbols, values), shapes the child's understanding of the meaning of his or her experiences.
- The curriculum can include practice in storytelling as a way to develop oral language skills and to make connections with children's real world experiences.
- Based on Gardner's work in multiple intelligences, children need more occasions to use music, bodily-kinesthetic, visual-spatial, and interpersonal domains to learn and express understanding. Brain research has indicated that the mental mechanism that processes music (and rhyme and rhythm) are deeply entwined with the brain's other basic functions, including emotion, perception, memory and even language. These mechanisms can be used to build social/emotional experiences in the classroom and to reinforce, memory, language development, or even mathematical skills. Children can also draw, paint, construct, and dramatize what they know and understand.
- It is the brain's principal job to ensure survival. The brain's emotional center is tied to its ability to learn. The amygdala checks all incoming sensory information first to see if it fits a known impression of danger. If a threat is perceived, the ability to learn is greatly impeded as the entire body automatically gears up to defend itself.
- Teachers have a central responsibility to create a learning environment that feels relaxed enough to allow children's attention to focus on the curriculum, and challenging enough to excite interest.
- Emotions, learning, and memory are closely linked as different parts of the brain are activated in the learning process. It is crucial to provide a rich and safe environment that lays groundwork for this neurological network to develop.
- Children need to explore, play, and discover, in a safe and healthy environment, using all of their senses in making connections from one part of the curriculum to another.

(Rushton and Larkin 2001)

TABLE 3.1 An overview of developmentally appropriate practices and connections between recent findings on brain research

NAEYC's DAP Position	Brain Research Principle	Classroom Environment
1. Domains of children's development—physical, social, emotional, and cognitive—are closely related. Development in one domain influences and is influenced by development in other domains.	Each brain region consists of highly sophisticated neurological network of cells, dendrites, and nerves that interconnect one portion of the brain to another. The brain's emotional center is tied to ability to learn. Emotions, learning, and memory are closely linked as different parts of the brain are activated in learning process.	Good curriculum engages many of the five senses and activates more than one of Gardner's nine intelligences at the same time. Learning is social activity. Children need opportunities to engage in dialogue. Multiage grouping is a strategy that can support and challenge a range of learning styles and capabilities. Good learning environments build trust, empower learners, and encourage students to explore their feelings and ideas.
2. Development occurs in a relatively orderly sequence, with later abilities, skills, and knowledge building on those already acquired.	The brain changes physiologically as a result of experience. New dendrites are formed every day, "hooking" new information to prior experiences. An enriched environment increases cell weight and branching of dendrites.	Hands-on activities stimulate the various regions of the brain, and active participation helps young children to form stronger associations with existing understanding. Different stages of play (solitary, parallel, associative, collaborative), can be identified, and appropriate activities designed to build increasingly complex ideas through play.
3. Development proceeds at varying rates from child to child as well as unevenly within different areas of a child's functioning.	Each brain is unique. Lock-step, assembly-line learning violates a critical discovery about the human brain: each brain is not only unique, but also is growing on its own timetable.	Environments should allow choices to accommodate a range of developmental styles and capabilities. Large blocks of time and systems for planning and tracking work, can be organized for children to share responsibility for their activity choices.

NAEYC's DAP Position	Brain Research Principle	Classroom Environment
		Teachers need to adjust expectations and performance standards to age-specific characteristics and unique capabilities of learners.
4. Early experiences have both cumulative and delayed effects on individual children's development. Optimal periods exist for certain types of development and learning.	Brain research indicates that certain "windows of opportunity" for learning do exist. The brain's "plasticity" allows for greater amounts of information to be processed and absorbed at certain critical periods (Wolfe 1998). The critical period for learning a spoken language is lost by about age 10 (Sorgen 1999).	Children need opportunities to use sensory inputs, language, and motor skills. Young children also require frequent opportunities to interact verbally with peers. Repeated opportunities to interact with materials, peers, and ideas are critical for long-term memory. Second language programs will be most successful before 5th grade and should start as early as possible.
5. Development proceeds in predictable directions toward greater complexity, organization, and internalization.	The brain is designed to perceive and generate patterns. The brain is designed to process many inputs at once and prefers multi-processing. Hence, a slower linear pace reduces understanding (Caine & Caine 1997).	Finding patterns can be built into math, language arts, science, and other subject area curriculum. Learning environments can be organized for both low and high order thinking skills. Use of metaphor, and repeated opportunities to compare and contrast through multiple modalities, allow children to differentiate increasingly complex schemas.
6. Children are active learners, drawing on direct physical and social experience as well as culturally transmitted knowledge to construct their own understanding of the world around them.	When a child is engaged in a learning experience, a number of areas of the brain are simultaneously activated. Children raised in non-academically oriented environments have little experience in using	Learning should be presented in a real-life context so new information builds upon prior understanding, and then generalizes to broader concepts. Field trips, guest speakers, interactive technology, and

NAEYC's DAP Position	Brain Research Principle	Classroom Environment
	decontextualized language. They are more inclined to reason with visual, hands-on strategies (Healy 1990).	multicultural units of study will help children better understand themselves and succeed in today's world.
7. Development and learning result from interaction of biological maturation and the environment, which includes both the physical and social worlds that children live in.	Each of the senses can be independently or collectively affected by environmental factors that in turn will affect the brain's ability to learn. Enriched environments increase dendritic branching and synaptic responses (Diamond 1998).	Environments should be carefully monitored for appropriate lighting, aromas, ionization (fresh air), and noise. Water and appropriate foods should be made available to children, remembering that each person's internal clock differs.
	The simple act of reading a book may be one of the most challenging tasks the brain must perform. Speech comes naturally, but reading does not (Sorgen, 1999).	Environments should offer a wealth of materials and activity choices to explore.

Children need to understand the relevance of learning to read. Learning to read should be connected to the child's speaking and writing. Reading aloud and reading for meaning are two different processes; children need opportunities to do both. |
| 8. Children demonstrate different modes of knowing and learning; and different ways of representing what they know. | "The mental mechanisms that process music (and rhyme and rhythm) are deeply entwined with the brain's other functions, including emotion, perception, memory, and even language" (Sorgen 1999, 56). | A classroom should provide opportunities for individual children to learn via modalities other than just verbal/linguistic or logical-mathematical tasks.

Rhyme and rhythm are memory aids. |
| | The most powerful influences on a learner's behavior are concrete, vivid images. The brain has a primitive response to pictures, symbols, and strong, simple images | Children should be able to express knowledge in a variety of forms. Dramatization, music, and the visual arts should be made readily available as modes of both learning and |

NAEYC's DAP Position	Brain Research Principle	Classroom Environment
	(Jenson 1995).	expression. Symbolic representation can easily be built into the arts.
9. Children develop and learn best in the context of a community where they are safe and valued, their physical needs are met, and they feel psychologically secure.	Brain research has clearly demonstrated that high levels of stress, or a perceived threat, will inhibit learning (Caine & Caine 1997). "The brain is primarily designed to survive. No intelligence or ability will unfold until or unless given the appropriate model environment" (Jensen 1996).	The classroom environment should connect learning experiences to positive emotions. Students need to make decisions and choices about learning that are meaningful to them. The classroom culture should support risk-taking, and view failures as a natural part of the learning process.

Source: Rushton and Larkin 2001, 25-33.

Development of Moral Character

"To educate a person in mind and not in morals is to educate a menace to society."
—Theodore Roosevelt (as cited in Lickona 1993).

As early as the 1800s some were concerned about development of character in individuals. It is reported that down through history, education has had two goals: to help people become smart and to help them become good. Therefore, character education is as old as education itself. It is reported that in the days of the republic, the Bible was the source book for moral and religious instruction. It was believed by philosophers and spiritual leaders that education should help individuals become "wise and good people." Because there was controversy over which Bible should be used, William McGuffey then developed his *McGuffey Readers* in 1836 as a way to teach school children the "natural virtues" of honesty, hard work, thriftiness, kindness, patriotism and courage. He sold more than 100 million copies. He retained many favorite biblical stories but added poems, exhortations, and heroic tales (Lickona 1993, 2006).

John Dewey, Emile Durkheim and Jean Piaget also were proponents of moral development. Dewey wrote *Moral Principles in Education* (1911) and Durkheim's book had a similar title, *Moral Education* (1925). This was followed by Hartshorne and May, *Studies in the Nature of Character* (1928-30) and Jean Piaget's work, *The Moral Judgment of the Child* (1932).

Even the work of C.S. Lewis addressed the issue of the good person, and attempted to provide a model. Lewis discovered that notions about character had been discussed worldwide and by many cultures. He reviewed the writings of the ancient Egyptians, Babylonians, Hebrews, Chinese, Norse, Indians, and Greeks; and Anglo-Saxon and American writings as well. The common values he found included such virtues as kindness; honesty; loyalty to parents, spouses, and family members; an obligation to help the poor, the sick, and the less fortunate; and the right to private property. Some evils, such as treachery, torture, and murder, were considered worse than one's own death (1947). Lewis called this universal path to becoming a good person by the Chinese name, 'the Tao." He believed that combining the wisdom of many cultures, this Tao could be the multicultural answer for how to live our lives and the basis for what is most worth knowing.

Beginning in the 20th century, focus on values and character began to diminish with discussions of Darwinism, evolution and the philosophy of logical positivism. Largely the discussion of values and morality became a private matter and not for transmission through the schools. It was not until the late 1960s and 1970s that there was a reemergence of values education in the schools with the focus on values clarification and Lawrence Kohlberg's work on the stages of moral reasoning and his moral dilemma discussions. In addition to outlining the developmental stages of moral reasoning in individuals, Kohlberg also sees moral education as stimulation for development (1966). This is an interesting assertion. He states:

> "The attractiveness of defining the goal of moral education as the stimulation of development rather than as teaching fixed virtues is that it means aiding the child to take the next step in a direction toward which he is already tending, rather than imposing an alien pattern upon him" (19).

Thomas Lickona, however, indicates that Kohlberg's theoretical limitation was that he focused on moral reasoning, which is necessary but not sufficient for good character; therefore, he underestimated the school's role as a moral socializer (1993).

In the 1990s, Thomas Lickona initiated the rebirth of the character education movement. He speaks of the importance of restoring the concept of "good character" to its historical place as the central desirable outcome of the school's moral enterprise. In July 1992, the Josephson Institute of

Ethics called together more than 30 educational leaders representing state school boards, teachers' unions, universities, ethics centers, youth organizations, and religious groups. They drafted the Aspen Declaration on Character Education, setting forth eight principles of character education. The National Character Education Partnership was launched in 1993 as a coalition whose goal was putting character development at the top of the nation's educational agenda. Members include representatives from business, labor, government, youth, parents, faith communities, and the media.

The Partnership provides a detailed philosophy and rationale for the reinstitution of character education in the schools, with some of the same reasons provided by his predecessors. Details of the principles and rationale can be found on the Character Education Partnership's website and in Lickona's article (1993). Most importantly, the basic tenets of character education encompass the cognitive, affective and behavioral aspects of morality. They indicate that good character consists of knowing the good, desiring the good, and doing the good. They believe that schools must help children understand the core values, adopt or commit to them, and then act upon them in their own lives.

The cognitive side of character includes at least 6 specific moral qualities: awareness of the moral dimensions of the situation at hand, knowing moral values and what they require of us in concrete cases, perspective-taking, moral reasoning, thoughtful decision-making, and moral self-knowledge. All of these powers of rational moral thought are required for full moral maturity and citizenship in a democratic society.

There also is an emotional side of character, which serves as the bridge between judgment and action. The emotional side includes at least the qualities of conscience (the felt obligation to do what one judges to be right, self-respect, empathy, loving the good, self-control, and humility (a willingness to both recognize and correct our moral failings).

Moral action is the third part of character and draws upon three additional moral qualities: competence (skills such as listening, communicating, and cooperating), will (which mobilizes our judgment and energy), and moral habit (a reliable inner disposition to respond to situations in a morally good way.

According to the Character Education Partnership, schools have an important role to play in using the classroom and school as deliberate tools of character development. Parents and schools have a responsibility to stand for good values and help students form their character around such values. A comprehensive approach to character education defines character to include its cognitive, emotional, and behavioral dimensions.

It seeks to provide students with repeated, real-life experiences that develop all three parts of character. It provides character building experiences for students through all phases of school life --formal and informal or hidden curriculum (Lickona 1993, 2006).

Ryan (1993) suggests that the formal curriculum could include stories, historical figures and events to illuminate the human condition. Curricula could also include interesting literature where students could learn about themselves and the world. For example, Ryan cites literature about *Harriet Tubman* where students come face-to-face with raw courage; *The Diary of Anne Frank*, where they learn to understand the danger of hate and racism; Edward Arlington Robinson's poem *"Miniver Cheevy"* where they learn the folly of storing up earthly treasures; Toni Cade Bambara's *"Your Blues Ain't Like Mine,"* where they learn the intrinsic dignity of each human being; or *To Kill A Mockingbird*, where they gain insight into the heart of a truly noble man, Atticus Finch; or Shakespeare's *Julius Caesar*, where they can perceive the thorny relationships between the leader and the led by following the well-intended, but failed efforts of Brutus.

The literature also cites the importance of developing moral imagination in children—the capacity to empathize with others. This means not to just feel for oneself, but to feel with and for others. Researchers have found that empathy training—including simple things as calling attention to less fortunate children or pointing out to a child that he or she has the power to make someone else happy by sharing—can increase young children's empathy scores and incidences of prosocial behavior (Cotton, 2006).

Figure 3.1 outlines a comprehensive approach as outlined by Lickona and the Partnership. Appendix A includes 100 ways to promote character education as compiled by the Center for the Advancement of Ethics and Character at Boston University; and examples of successful programs and their focus.

Enriching the Lives of Children 27

Figure 3.1 12-Point Comprehensive Approach to Character Education

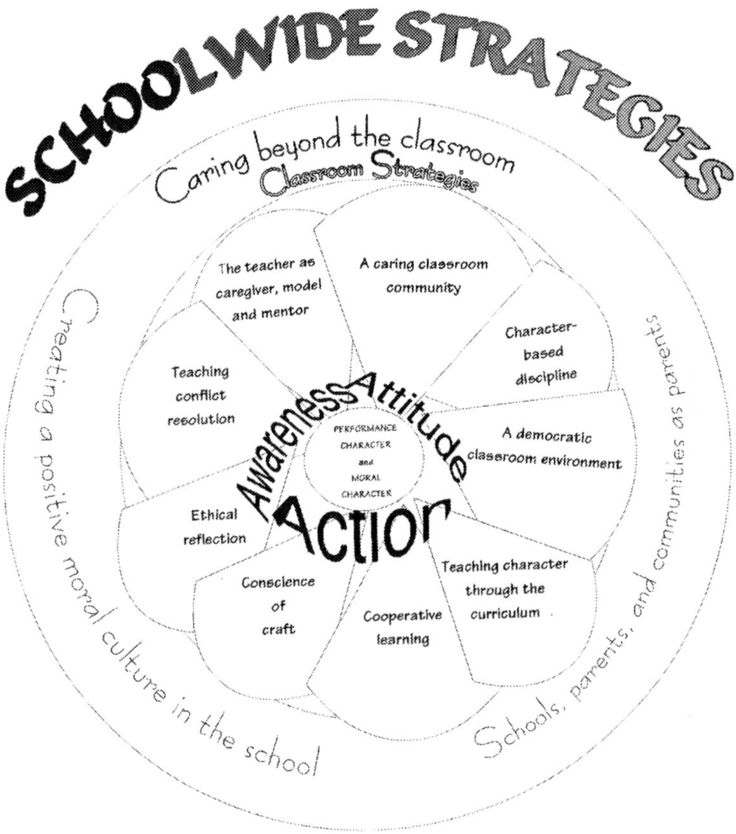

Source: Center for the 4th & 5th Rs-Respect and Responsibility. Online at: http://www.cortland.edu/character/12pts.asp

Stimulating Emotional Development

As indicated earlier, all of the developmental domains are interdependent. Therefore, emotional development is related to cognitive development and to moral development. The work of Damasio points out the fact that moral behaviors are emotional—such as the expression of compassion, shame, indignation, dominant pride or submission. The contribution of everything that is learned and created in a group plays a major role in shaping moral behaviors. (Damasio 2006). In addition, emotions are brain representations of body states. Patterns in the external world correspond with patterns of nerve cell activity in the brain, and these brain patterns are termed cognitive representations. Therefore, 'thinking' is carried out by means of patterns of nerve cell activation. Damasio suggests that while the senses of vision, hearing, touch, taste and smell function by nerve activation patterns that correspond to the state of the external world; emotions are nerve activation patterns that correspond to the state of the internal world. If we experience a state of fear, for example, then our brains will record this body state in nerve cell activation patterns obtained from neural and hormonal feedback; and this information may then be used to adapt behavior appropriately. Emotions are vital to the higher reaches of distinctively human intelligence. Contrary to some popular notions, emotions do not 'get in the way of' rational thinking – emotions are essential to rationality (Charlton 2006, Damasio 1999).

Moreover, stimulating educational experiences can trigger the sensory and emotional states of individuals in positive or negative ways. According to one model, Kurt Fischer's "skill theory" (1980), as summarized by Suizzo (2000), emotions are generated in human beings through the appraisal of events in relation to specific goals (Fischer, Shaver, & Carnochan 1990). These emotions then generate actions and "action tendencies" that are appropriate both to our particular cultural models and to our personal histories or "scripts." As children develop, this constant interplay between their cognitive and emotional functions gives rise to increases in their abilities to reflect on and understand their emotions, consider others' perspectives, and inhibit or plan their actions. Fischer's research on children's development has shown that a child's performance level on a given cognitive task will vary according to the level of social support he or she is accorded. With support, modeling or prompting, children are able to perform at their optimal level. Without such support, they rarely perform at their optimal level but more at their 'functional' level; and, show no evidence of competence at the higher level. Thus, in assessing where children are cognitively, teachers should include high support conditions. Supporting this model is Lev Vygotsky's concept of the 'zone of proximal development' and the use of scaffolding as a positive technique when providing instruction to students, both for learning and cognitive development. According to Vygotsky, the zone of proximal development occurs when a less skilled person learns in collaboration with more skilled individuals. According to Vygotsky (1931/1998), it is only through knowing others that one comes to know oneself: "If the thought of the child did not meet with the thoughts of others, the child would never become conscious of himself" (72, as cited by Moran and John-Steiner, 2003).

Also, several Francophone neo-Piagetian scholars, such as Mina Verba and Fajda Winnykamen (1992) have examined the role of social and emotional factors of children's performance on problem-solving tasks, both alone and in cooperative contexts, to assess the effects of social interaction on cognitive performance. These researchers find that individual performance level is influenced by the particular dynamic of the dyad, which is in turn shaped by factors such as the individual's status within the dyad (Berzin, Cauzinille & Winnykamen 1995; Verba & Winnykamen 1992), self-reported feelings of self-efficacy (Puustinen & Winnykamen 1998), and degree of sociability (DaSilva & Winnykamen 1998).

There is also much in the literature on the cultural contexts of social, emotional, and cognitive development. The research literature points to the fact that development is dependent upon the cultural perspectives of a group, and what any given culture may consider valued or they know and use, or not valued or what they do not know and use.

Likewise, students can bring negative emotions to the classroom that can impede their ability to learn. Daniel Goleman has developed the concept of emotional intelligence that is related to this fact. He defines emotional intelligence as the way one handles their own feelings, and how well they are able to empathize and get along with other people. He also indicates that the state of the person's emotional base can impact in positive or negative ways the outcomes on performance and achievement. According to Goleman, children who are better able to manage their emotions, can actually pay attention better, take in information better and remember better. Having positive emotional grounding helps the child to learn better (2006). According to Goleman, it is the mission of schools to socialize children and prepare them for life. It also involves teaching children how to manage themselves better, how to handle rocky emotions, how to handle other people, how to cooperate and get along with others. Goleman believes that teachers are the critical models for children in the classroom by the behaviors that they model. Teachers can expand their emotional-social repertoire of understanding and their reactions; and children can learn from this just through their observations of teachers. Emotional development in the classroom is part of the implicit curriculum—learning how to get along with other people, learning how to motivate one's self, learning how to persist, how to resist temptation and stay fixed on a goal, and how to work together toward a common goal.

Cooperative learning, according to Goleman and others, is a wonderful natural laboratory for children to acquire a set of skills absolutely essential for life. It is imperative that schools practice cooperative learning because families are not using it the way they use to, and seem not to be able to do it as well. Goleman asserts that school then is the only place we can be sure that every child has a chance to learn it. Through cooperative learning children learn how to manage themselves, how to get along with other people, how to handle anger, and more. Furthermore, the group can exert pressure, forcing children to want to learn how to get along better (Goleman 2006).

Thus, educators and policymakers are discovering the importance of social and emotional variables in academic performance and achievement. As a result, they are placing their attention on methods and practices that foster students' social and emotional development, and on managing emotions that interfere with learning and concentration. There are now social and emotional learning (SEL) programs, whose aim is to promote the social and emotional competence of children and their capacity to recognize and manage emotions, solve problems effectively, and establish and maintain positive relationships with others (Ragozzino, Resnik, Utne-OBrien, and Weissberg 2003). A substantial body of research supports the notion that social and emotional variables are integral rather than incidental to learning (Wang, Jaertel, and Walbert 1997). Furthermore, in a meta-analysis of 165 studies by Wilson, Gottfredson, and Najaka (2001), where they examined the effectiveness of various school-based prevention activities, they found that social and emotional learning programs increased attendance and decreased the dropout rate. Furthermore, a study by Zins et al. (n.d.) found that SEL programs improved student attitudes, behaviors and academic performance.

Social and emotional learning programs then, seem to provide students with basic skills for success, not just in school but also in their personal, professional and civic lives. The Collaborative for Academic, Social, and Emotional Learning (CASEL), an organization working to establish SEL as an essential part of P-12 education has identified specific ways in which SEL programs positively affect academic performance. These approaches can be found on their website at: www.CASEL.org.

Creativity and Development

In discussing enriching the lives of children using novel and meaningful stimulus experiences, it would be remiss to have this discussion without including a look at creativity and its relationship to development. While creativity is a relatively new field and much is still being understood about the nature of creativity, it was the focus of earlier discussions by Lev Vygotsky and others; and is currently being reexamined and redefined by a group of scholars who include Sawyer, Gardner, Feldman, Sternberg, Csikszentmihalyi and others.

Creativity is included in the developmental domain and interrelated to cognitive and emotional development. Children's play in early childhood is said to also contribute to creative endeavors; and leads to further potential for creativity as one continues growth and development throughout the lifespan. Many early scholars suggested that artistic activity and children's play are related and in some way tap into the same inner source. It is reported that in the centuries prior to the modern era, this inner source was often viewed as divine inspiration; and, children were thought to be closer to God (Sawyer, et al. 2003).

Other scholars also correlated creativity to children's play. It is indicated that German idealists such as Schiller (1793, 1794, and 1968) associated the creative impulse with children's play, and almost since the beginning of formal schooling, idealists and romanticists alike have criticized overly structured classroom schooling for squashing children's natural creative ability. Others in the twentieth century, such as Freud, also indicated that the artist was like a child at play. According to Freud's description, *"he [the artist] creates a world of his own, or rather, re-arranges the things of his world in a new way which pleases him"* (Freud, 1907/1989, 437, as cited in Sawyer et al. 2003, 4). For Freud, fantasy worlds are created by both the child and the artist from the same motivating impulse: the desire to satisfy an unfulfilled wish (439).

One of the main questions asked in the research being conducted on creativity and development is: Are children more creative than adults? This question has been addressed by many indicating that creativity is largely a developmental and transitional process. Many do believe, however, that pretend play in childhood is a precursor to creativity (Singer & Singer 1990; Smolucha 1992; Russ 1996; Sawyer 1997).

There have also been different foci relative to defining creativity over the decades. The first wave of creativity research from the 1950s to the 1970s came from the perspective of personality psychology and focused primarily on psychometrics, the development of instruments to measure creativity and the identification of traits and components of creativity by domain. By the 1970s, it is reported that the aim was to develop metrics that could aid in identifying exceptional creative talent in childhood, to those more likely to succeed in occupations demanding creativity (Sawyer et al. 2003). The Terman studies, looking at the gifted and talented in the

1920s and tracking their development into adulthood, also examined creativity from a longitudinal perspective.

There were also shifts in the focus of creativity studies, from personality to process. Moreover, there was an increasing interest in the mental processes that underlie exceptional ability and everyday problem-solving and decision-making. Further, the constructivist's notions and the work of Piaget and Vygotsky added much to the paradigm on creativity. Later contemporary educational theory also is based on the constructivist insight that children create their own knowledge. In this framework, according to Sawyer, educators must be centrally concerned with creative processes, because they cannot simply teach students knowledge but rather must create the environmental conditions that will enable children to construct their own knowledge.

Moreover, there is much discussion about the parallels between the processes of creativity and development and the concept of novelties and the interrelationships (Sawyer et al. 2003). A major question is: what are novelties and how do you explain them? Further, how do novelties occur in development and how do children make the constructive and creative transition to the next conceptual stage? Sawyer believes that *novelties are creations that constantly intervene in development* (6). Another critical question raised relative to creativity is: what is the relationship between the creative process and the role of social interaction that lead to the development of a creative product?

There have been many explanations offered relative to a definition of creativity: that it is *"a socially recognized achievement in which there are novel products"* (Barron & Harrington, 1981, p.442); *"that creativity is a function of both the individual and selective environment"* (Csikszentmihalyi 1988); *'that creativity is at heart, a developmental process, it is transformational"* (Feldman 2003). Early on, Lev Vygotsky defined creativity as *"a social and individual process"* (Moran and John-Steiner, 2003). Creativity transforms both the creator, through the personal experience of the process, and others, through the impact of new knowledge and innovative artifacts disseminated through culture (Moran and John Steiner 2003).

Lev Vygotsky's early writings are now being considered a significant contribution to developing a clearer understanding to the field of creativity studies. Several researchers have spent a significant amount of time reviewing Vygotsky's theories and writings about the creative imagination. Moran and John-Steiner (2003) make some of the following points about the views of Vygotsky from his writings:

- Vygotsky believed that creative work is profoundly social. He indicated that: *"Art is the social within us ....Art is the social technique of emotion, a tool of society which brings the most intimate and personal aspects of our being into the circle of social life...."* (249).
- Vygotsky conceived of developmental and creative processes as *internalization* or appropriation of cultural tools and social interaction. Internalization is not just copying but rather a transformation or reorganization of incoming information and mental structures based on the individual's characteristics and existing knowledge.
- Creative imagination is necessary for effective functioning in society. People with a less developed creative imagination cannot remove themselves from the immediate stimuli of the environment.
- Vygotsky also theorized that children first learn to create and manipulate symbols and signs during play. He stated that children's pretend play and object substitution become internalized as fantasy or imagination as inner speech develops. In adolescence, creative imagination results when imagination and thinking in concepts become conjoined. This, in adulthood, can mature into artistic and scientific creativity.
- Vygotsky thought that children first learn to create, manipulate, and give meaning to signs and symbols through play. Play also allows children to tease out relationships, try on and practice different roles, and exercise their growing capabilities (Vygotsky, 1984, 1999).
- Pretend play starts with social interaction with adults: Somebody first shows a child how a banana can be a phone, or how a broom can be a dancing partner. (Smolucha & Smolucha, 1986).
- Over time and experience, children become more adventurous, as make-believe objects move further from their real-world characters. As children reach school age, goals and rules become a focus of play, and play becomes an early mechanism for self-mastery. Vygotsky also believed that a child's greatest self-control occurs in play (1978).
- Through play, children can scaffold their own learning, creating a zone of proximal development between their present level of achievement and their more competent future selves. By practicing skills or trying out ideas within a play situation, children become better able to handle real situations (Sawyer, 1997).
- Creative imagination emerges when fantasy becomes infused with thinking in concepts. Then, imagination and the ability to abstract and categorize become integrated into a functional system (Vygotsky 1931/1998).

- Vygotsky traced the origins of the creative imagination to children's symbolic play. According to Vygotsky, once play is internalized, it forms the basis of fantasy, which develops further when linked to inner speech. In adolescence, imagination is fueled by the intense needs and emotions of the young, but also becomes closely linked to thinking concepts or becomes "intellectualized."
- Development of the creative imagination, then, is based on what is usually considered creative activity: pretend play, fantasy, and the making of creative products.
- Underpinning creativity is the conscious awareness of the interaction of one's own and others' subjective, emotional experiences. The sharing of emotions through art does not mean that each individual experiences that emotion in the same manner; each internalizes the experience through his or her own lens and background (Vygotsky, 1959/1987).
- According to Vygotsky, meaning relates emotion to activity and activity to emotion by way of a complex process of shared understanding. Meaning is the socially agreed-on definition of something—the dictionary definition for a word, for example. Creativity involves bringing something new into the realm of social meaning (1930/1997, 111).
- Vygotsky believed that "every inventor, even a genius, is always the outgrowth of his time and environment. His creativity stems from those needs that were created before him, and rests upon those possibilities that, again, exist outside of him." (1987).
- Creativity results in the proliferation of culture: "In the process of historical development, social man changes the methods and devices of his behavior...and develops and creates new forms of behavior—specifically cultural" (Vygotsky, 1960/1997, p.18).

Robert Sternberg (2003) has developed an *investment theory of creativity*. He believes that creative people are willing and able to buy low and sell high in the realm of ideas. Buying low means pursuing ideas that are unknown or out of favor but have growth potential. Often when these ideas are first presented, they encounter resistance. The creative individual persists in the face of this resistance and eventually sells high, moving on to the next new or unpopular idea.

According to Sternberg, evidence abounds illustrating that creative ideas are often rejected. He cites examples of many talented individuals whose initial reviews were often negative, such as Toni Morrison, Sylvia Plath, Edvard Munch, John Garcia and others. From this perspective, Sternberg indicates that the creative person buys low by presenting an idea that initially is not valued and then attempts to convince other people of its value. Sternberg also indicates that creativity is often obvious in young children. However, it may be harder to find in older children and adults because their creative potential has been suppressed by a society that encourages intellectual conformity.

He also defines ways that teachers and parents can promote creative performance in children. Sternberg believes that teachers and parents can encourage their children to define and redefine their own problems and projects. Adults can encourage creative thinking by having children choose their own topics for papers or presentations, choose their own ways of solving problems, and sometimes having them choose again if they discover their selection was a mistake. Sternberg asserts that giving children latitude in making choices helps them to develop taste and good judgment, both which are essential elements of creativity.

Teachers and parents can help children develop this talent by making questioning a part of the daily exchange. It is more important for children to learn what questions to ask—and how to ask them—than to learn the answers. Sternberg goes on to outline 21 ways to help children develop creativity. Table 3.2 lists Sternberg's suggestions for encouraging creativity.

TABLE 3.2 Sternberg's 21 Ways to Encourage Creativity in Children

Recommendation	Explanation
1. **Redefine the Problem**	Teachers and parents can promote creative performance by encouraging their children to define and redefine their own problems and projects. Adults can encourage creative thinking by having children choose their own topics for papers or presentations (subject to adults approval), choose their own ways of solving problems, and sometimes having them choose again if they discover their selection was a mistake.
2. **Question and Analyze Assumptions**	Creative people question assumptions and eventually lead others to do the same. Questioning assumptions is part of the analytical thinking involved in creativity. Teachers and parents can help children develop this talent by making questioning a part of the daily exchange. It is more important for children to learn what questions to ask—and how to ask them—than to learn the answers.

3. Do Not Assume that Creative Ideas Sell Themselves: Sell Them	Children need to learn how to persuade other people of the value of their ideas. This selling is part of the practical aspect of creative thinking. If children do science projects, it is a good idea for them to present those and demonstrate why they make important contributions.
4. Encourage Idea Generation	Creative people demonstrate a legislative style of thinking: they like to generate ideas. Children should be praised for generating ideas, regardless of whether some are silly or unrelated, while being encouraged to identify and develop their best ideas into high-quality projects.
5. Recognize that Knowledge is a Double-Edged Sword and Act Accordingly	One cannot be creative without knowledge. Those with a greater knowledge base can be creative in ways that those who are still learning about the basics of the field cannot be.
6. Encourage Children to Identify and Surmount Obstacles	Buying low and selling high means defying the crowd. And people who defy the crowd—people who think creatively—almost inevitably encounter resistance. When children attempt to surmount obstacles, they should be praised for the effort, whether or not they are entirely successful. Having the class brainstorm about ways to confront a given obstacle can get the class thinking about the many strategies people can use to confront problems.
7. Encourage Sensible Risk-Taking	Few children are willing to take risks in school, because they learn that taking risks can be costly. Perfect test scores and papers receive praise and open up future possibilities. Failure to attain a certain academic standard is perceived as deriving from a lack of ability and motivation and may lead to scorn and lessened opportunities. Why risk taking hard courses or saying things that teachers may not like when that may lead to low grades or even failure? Teachers may inadvertently advocate children's only learning to play it safe when they give assignments without choices and allow only particular answers to questions. Teachers need to encourage sensible risk-taking and reward it.

8. Encourage Tolerance of Ambiguity	A creative idea tends to come in bits and pieces and develop over time. The period in which the idea is developing tends to be uncomfortable. Without time or the ability to tolerate ambiguity, many may jump to a less than optimal solution. When a student has almost the right topic for a paper or almost the right science project, it is tempting for teachers to accept the near miss. To help children become creative, teachers need to encourage them to accept and extend the period during which their ideas do not quite converge. Children need to be taught that uncertainty and discomfort are a part of living a creative life. Ultimately, they will benefit from their tolerance of ambiguity by coming up with better ideas.
9. Help Children Build Self-Efficacy	Many people eventually reach a point at which they feel as if no one believes in them. Because creative work often does not get a warm reception, it is extremely important that creative people believe in the value of what they are doing. Sometimes teachers and parents unintentionally limit what children can do by sending messages that express or imply limits on their potential accomplishments. Instead, these adults need to help children believe in their own ability to be creative.
10. Help Children Find What They Love to Do	To help children uncover their true interests, teachers can ask them to demonstrate special talents or abilities for the class and explain that it does not matter what they do (within reason), only that they love the activities they choose.
11. Teach Children the Importance of Delaying Gratification	People are often ignored when they do creative work or even punished for doing it. By working on a task for many weeks or months, children learn the value of making incremental efforts for long-term gains.
12. Model Creativity	Children develop creativity when they are shown how.
13. Cross-Fertilize Ideas	Teachers should help students think across subjects and disciplines. Cross-fertilization motivates children who are not interested in subjects taught in the abstract.
14. Allow Time for Creative Thinking	If children are asked to think creatively, they need time to do it well.

15. **Instruct and Assess for Creativity**	If a teacher gives only multiple-choice tests, children quickly learn that the teacher values memorization and correct answers. If teachers want to encourage creativity, they need to include at least some opportunities for creative thought in assignments and tests. Questions that require factual recall, analytic thinking, and creative thinking should be asked.
16. **Reward Creativity**	If the goal of assessment is to instruct children, then it is better to ask for creative work and evaluate it with somewhat less objectivity than to evaluate children exclusively on uncreative work. Teachers should let children know that there is no completely objective way to evaluate creativity.
17. **Allow Mistakes**	Schools are often unforgiving of mistakes. Children learn that it is not all right to make mistakes. The result is that they become afraid to risk the independent and sometimes flawed thinking that leads to creativity. When children make mistakes, teachers should ask them to analyze and discuss these mistakes.
18. **Teach Children to Take Responsibility for Successes and Failures**	Teaching children how to take responsibility means teaching children to a) understand their creative process, b) criticize themselves, and c) take pride in their best creative work.
19. **Encourage Creative Collaboration**	Teachers can encourage children to learn by example by collaborating with creative people.
20. **Teach Children to Imagine Things from Others' Points of View**	Teachers and parents should encourage children to see the importance of understanding, respecting, and responding to other people's points of view.
21. **Maximize Person-Environment Fit**	Teachers should prepare their students to choose environments that are conducive to their creative success. Encourage children to examine environments to help them learn to select and match environments with their skills.

Source: Sternberg 2003, 118-130.

Sternberg believes that by encouraging students to think creatively—to create, imagine, suppose, discover, invent—teachers can help students improve their achievement. Some students already do these things and typically are not reinforced or even may be punished by their schools. Teachers can reconstruct classrooms so that deciding for creativity is rewarded rather than punished, resulting in improved student achievement.

Citing empirical evidence, Sternberg reports on a study where he and associates examined the learning of social studies and science by third and eighth graders using three instructional modalities. The sample included 225 third graders from a low income neighborhood in Raleigh, North Carolina; and 142 eight graders from middle to upper middle class areas in Baltimore, Maryland and Fresno, California. Students were assigned to one of three instructional conditions: 1) instruction was dependent on memory; 2) instruction was dependent on critical (analytical) thinking; and 3) a combination of strategies--analytical, creative and practical thinking. All students' performance was assessed for memory learning (through multiple-choice assessments) as well as for analytical, creative, and practical learning (through performance assessments).

They found that students in the condition that encouraged a mix of analytical, creative, and practical thinking outperformed the other students. Therefore, Sternberg and associates concluded that teaching for diverse modes of thinking is superior. It enables children to capitalize on their strengths and to correct or to compensate for their weaknesses; and, it allows children to encode material in a variety of interesting ways. Other studies have expanded Sternberg's initial study and expanded the subject areas and the number of students. These studies also had similar findings: that students who are taught triarchically substantially outperformed students who were taught in standard ways (see Grigorenko, Jarvin, & Sternberg, 2002). Based on this evidence, Sternberg concludes that our goal in school should be to teach in a way that makes deciding for creativity normative rather than counter normative.

PART FOUR

STRUCTURES AND STRATEGIES FOR CREATING NOVEL STIMULUS EXPERIENCES

Educating the Whole Child

More recently, there is a call to focus more on educating the whole child. This call has come from "progressive educators." In a national study on public schools in the late 1970s, John Goodlad (1979) concluded that public education should educate the whole child and avoid rote teaching that may raise test scores but fail to produce healthy, fulfilled, and participating citizens.

What does it mean to educate the whole child? It is the call for paying attention to not only the intellectual side of children, but to their emotional and social development as well. *"To neglect the social and emotional aspects of their development, to focus all our attention on measured academic performance, is to blind us to these youngsters' need to live a satisfying life"* (Eisner, 2005). In addition, this call for holistic education also focuses on the physical development of children.

Educators are calling for creating an environment that recognizes the distinctive talents that individual children possess and actualizing their potentialities. The Association for Supervision and Curriculum Development (ASCD) has a position statement on the whole child. Part of the statement asserts:

"ASCD believes a comprehensive approach to learning recognizes that successful young people are knowledgeable, emotionally and physically healthy, motivated, civically inspired, engaged in the arts, prepared for work and economic self-sufficiency, and ready for the world beyond their own borders" (Eisner 2005,18.)

Would this be a paradigm shift for schools? Many educators believe that the approach to education should be holistic—by looking at the whole child and developing strategies which would support all the developmental domains and the growth and development of the human person.

Armstrong (2007) advocates for a human development curriculum that is environmentally sensitive to the ecologies of different developmental stages of life. This curriculum would extend beyond basic skills and include the arts, physical education, social skills training, and imaginative, moral and spiritual development. By focusing on the whole child, it is believed that society can prepare students to meet the challenges of the real world in the years ahead.

Teaching for Multiple Intelligences

Howard Gardner's theory of multiple intelligences sparked a scientific revolution in cognitive psychology and in classrooms around the world. His revolutionary paradigm is described as "a mutiny against the notion that human beings have a single, fixed intelligence" (Checkley 1997). It is reported that the fervor with which educators embraced his premise that we have multiple intelligences, surprised even Gardner, himself. Today, if you conduct an internet search of "multiple intelligences," one is likely to find at least several thousand websites, schools and programs based on Gardner's theory.

Gardner's definition of intelligence is culturally relevant and includes products as an end result. In Gardner's words, "intelligence refers to the human ability to solve problems or to make something that is valued in one or more cultures." (Gardner, as cited in Checkley 1997). Therefore, the end result of intelligence is the types of products one can produce.

Gardner also asks some other questions about intelligence and says that the ability must meet some other criteria. For example, he raises the following questions: Is there a particular representation in the brain for the ability? Are there populations that are especially good or especially impaired in an intelligence? And, can an evolutionary history of intelligence be seen in animals other than human beings? Gardner believes his eight intelligences fit the criteria.

Gardner's theory of multiple intelligences, challenges the old notions about IQ. The old paradigm largely had limited views of an individual's capabilities, measured only by school performance and including only measures of linguistic, logical-mathematical, and occasionally spatial ability. As Gardner indicates, school matters, but only insofar as it yields something that can be used once students leave school. Therefore, school is responsible for helping students discover and develop their talents or strengths.

According to Gardner, what the old intelligence tests and models did not do was to inform about other intelligences that a person may have.

Further, they did not recognize other virtues like creativity or civic mindedness, or whether a person is moral or ethical (Checkley 1997). Thus, Gardner's IQ analytical model actually expands the capabilities of man for the first time since J.P. Guilford's attempt with his 120 unique abilities. Table 4.1 provides an overview of Gardner's 8 intelligences in his own words.

Teachers are interpreting Gardner's MI theory into practice in the classroom. They are planning projects, lessons, assessments, apprenticeships and interdisciplinary curricula programs based on his theory. In an article by Linda Campbell on how MI theory is being translated in the classroom, she outlines a variety of programs and strategies using Gardner's paradigm. Campbell cites 5 structured ways that MI theory was found to be used in the classroom: in lesson designs, interdisciplinary curriculums, student projects, assessments, and apprenticeships.

In developing lesson designs, many teachers use the multiple intelligences as entry points into lesson content. In addition, many teachers would ask students to select the ways they would like to learn. She cites a case about teachers who are having students rotate learning stations as is the case in a classroom at Tulalip Elementary School. She points to teachers at Wheeler Elementary School in Louisville, Kentucky who plan and teach in teams based on their own intelligence strengths. Each teacher assumes responsibility for two intelligences and contributes to his or her grade level curriculum accordingly. Students then rotate from classroom to classroom, learning from three or four teachers for each unit of study. When interviewed, students have said they appreciate the hands-on nature of their learning and each teacher's enthusiasm (Campbell 1997).

Some secondary teachers capitalize on multiple intelligence theory by coordinating school wide interdisciplinary units. Gardner cautions, however, that teachers should possess the knowledge of the individual disciplines.

Educators also use the theory to promote self-directed learning. They prepare students for their adult lives by teaching them how to initiate and manage complex projects. Students learn to ask researchable questions; to identify varied resources; to create realistic time lines; and to initiate, implement and bring closure to a learning activity (Campbell 1997). It is reported that even primary age children can learn how to execute projects. With teacher guidance, students at Project Spectrum, Howard Gardner's lab school at Harvard—study local birds and their nesting habits. They design and build bird houses and then observe whether their designs successfully meet the needs of the birds or whether modifications are needed. Some teachers encourage students to identify their own topics to pursue for classroom projects. Many teachers also develop a set of guidelines for students to follow in conducting their projects.

According to Campbell, teachers should reflect on a concept they want to teach and identity the intelligences that seem most appropriate for communicating the content. She offers instructional menus, based on Gardner's MI theory, which teachers could draw from for classroom activities. Table 4.2 presents her recommendations.

It is recommended that teachers evaluate projects and other coursework by designing assessments that can demonstrate students' higher order thinking skills and where they can generalize what they have learned, provide examples, connect content to personal experiences and apply their knowledge to new situations (Campbell 1997). An exemplary case cited was that of teachers at Eleanor Roosevelt Elementary School in Vancouver, Washington. They developed an assessment approach that involves both parents and students. Students evaluate the skills and knowledge they have acquired and include their assessments in their portfolios. They also work in groups to assess one another's projects and evaluate their courses and teachers. Parents participate by setting goals and assessing with their children by reviewing student videotapes, by evaluating courses and by writing informal comments during their visits to the classroom. It is reported that these types of assessments yield more comprehensive pictures of student progress while giving students and parents a stronger voice in schooling (Campbell 1997).

Gardner also suggests that schools personalize their programs for students by offering them apprenticeships during their elementary and secondary school years. The apprenticeships would not track students into careers at an early age, but would contribute to a well-rounded liberal arts education and consume approximately one-third of students' schooling experience. It is recommended that each student participate in three apprenticeships: one in an art form or craft, one in an academic area, and a third in a physical discipline such as dance or sports. Students would have input into which apprenticeships they pursued. These programs could be offered as part of the regular school curriculum or as extracurricular enrichment opportunities.

At the Key School in Indianapolis—the first multiple intelligences school in the U.S.—teachers, parents, and community members mentor students in 17 crafts or disciplines—each one called a "pod." Each student attends a pod, of his or her choice, four times a week to work on material related to one or more intelligences. Because each pod is open to any student in the school, children of varying ages participate in each of them. Pod topics include architecture, cooking, and gardening; as well as themes called Sing and Song, Logo writer, Imagine Indianapolis (city planning), and Young Astronauts. In addition, a local museum offers Key students apprenticeships in shipbuilding, journalism, animation, or weather monitoring. These programs offer students powerful opportunities to work with older students or adults who have achieved competence in a discipline or craft. And, according to program developers, when students are immersed in real-world tasks, students begin to see where their efforts may lead (Campbell 1997, Key School 2006).

There also is evidence that MI theory has been successful in many school programs, nationally and globally. For example, one teacher used MI theory with special needs children with much success (Merrefield, 1997). A Maryland elementary school teacher introduced MI theory in the Maryland Public Schools and found the innovations to improve children's performance on state tests and create a school wide culture of achievement (Greenhawk 1997).

Based on a survey of 30 schools in Australia, MI theory has transformed teaching in Australia, especially among preschool, primary school, and special educators. Further, these schools have reported that gifted education has been enriched as well. In particular, MI theory broadened educators' views of giftedness and led teachers to more frequently identify giftedness in students from disadvantaged groups. Beyond the classroom, the theory is widely used in training programs in business and industry. One of the most significant changes cited was a shift from teacher-centered to student-centered activities in the classroom. Students participate in mutually planning, implementing, observing, and reflecting on their work; and students can develop their own independent projects (Vialle 1997).

Finally, the Charlotte-Mecklenburg school district used MI theory to revamp their educational program for the gifted. They developed activities that call for rigorous content, thinking and research skills that engage students and help them develop thoughtful, intellectual, and even scholarly dispositions. They indicate that MI theory has helped them recognize students' strengths, and teachers are better able to shape classrooms that truly engage children's curiosity and enable them to learn and create in many ways (Reid and Romanoff 1997).

TABLE 4.1 Overview of Multiple Intelligences From Howard Gardner

Gardner's Overview of His Theory of Multiple Intelligences

- **Linguistic Intelligence** – The capacity to use language, your native language, and perhaps other languages to express what's on your mind and to understand other people. Poets really specialize in linguistic intelligence, but any kind of writer, orator, speaker, lawyer, or a person for whom language is an important stock in trade highlights linguistic intelligence.

- **Logical-Mathematical Intelligence** – People with highly developed logical mathematical intelligence understand the underlying principles of some kind of a causal system, the way a scientist or a logician does; or can manipulate numbers, quantities, and operations, the way a mathematician does.

- **Spatial Intelligence** – The ability to represent the spatial world internally in your mind—the way a sailor or airplane pilot navigates the large spatial world, or the way a chess player or sculptor represents a more circumscribed spatial world. Spatial intelligence can be used in the arts or in the sciences. If you are spatially intelligent and oriented toward the arts, you are more likely to become a painter or a sculptor, architect, musician or writer. Also certain sciences like anatomy or topology emphasize spatial intelligence.

- **Bodily-Kinesthetic Intelligence** – The capacity to use your whole body or parts of your body—your hand, fingers, arms—to solve a problem, make something, or put on some kind of a production. The most evident examples are people in athletics of the performing arts, such as dance or acting.

- **Musical Intelligence** – The capacities to think in music, to be able to hear patterns, recognize them, remember them, and perhaps manipulate them. People who have strong musical intelligence don't just remember music easily, they can not get it out of their minds, it's omnipresent.

- **Interpersonal Intelligence** – Understanding other people. It is an ability we all need, but is at a premium if you are a teacher, clinician, salesperson, or politician. Anyone who deals with other people has to be skilled in the interpersonal sphere.

- **Intrapersonal Intelligence** – Refers to having an understanding of yourself, of knowing who you are, what you can do, what you want to do, how you react to things, which things to avoid, and which things to gravitate toward. We are drawn to people who have a good understanding of themselves because those people tend not to screw up. They tend to know what they can do. They tend to know what they can not do. And they tend to know where to go if they need help.

- **Naturalist Intelligence** – Designates the human ability to discriminate among living things (plants, animals) as well as sensitivity to other features of the natural world (clouds, rock configurations). This ability was clearly of value in our evolutionary past as hunters, gatherers, and farmers; it continues to be central in such roles as botanist or chef. I also speculate that much of our consumer society exploits the naturalists' intelligences, which can be mobilized in the discrimination among cars, sneakers, kinds of makeup, and the like. The kind of pattern recognition valued in certain of the sciences may also draw upon naturalist intelligence.

Source: Checkley 1997, Conversation with Howard Gardner.

TABLE 4.2 Multiple Intelligences Menus

Linguistic Menu	Musical Menu
Use storytelling to explain____ Conduct a debate on____ Write a poem, myth, legend, short play or news article about____ Create a talk show radio program about____ Conduct an interview of ____on____	Give a presentation with appropriate musical accompaniment on____ Sing a rap or song that explains____ Indicate the rhythmical patterns in____ Explain how the music of a song is similar to____ Make an instrument and use it to demonstrate____
Logical-Mathematical Menu	**Interpersonal Menu**
Translate a ____ into a mathematical formula Design and conduct an experiment on____ Make up syllogisms to demonstrate____ Make up analogies to explain____ Describe the patterns or symmetry in ____ Others of your choice____	Conduct a meeting to address____ Intentionally use ____ social skills to learn about____ Participate in a service project to____ Teach someone about____ Practice giving and receiving feedback on____ Use technology to____
Bodily-Kinesthetic Menu	**Intrapersonal Menu**
Create a movement or sequence of movements to explain____ Make task or puzzle cards for____ Build or construct a ____ Plan and attend a field trip that will____ Bring hands-on materials to demonstrate____	Describe qualities you possess that will help you successfully complete____ Set and pursue a goal to____ Describe one of your personal values about____ Write a journal entry on____ Assess your own work in____
Visual Menu	**Naturalist Menu**
Chart, map, cluster, or graph____ Create a slide show, videotape, or photo album of____ Create a piece of art that demonstrates____ Invent a board or card game to demonstrate____ Illustrate, draw, paint, sketch, or sculpt____	Create observation notebooks of____ Describe changes in the local or global environment____ Care for pets, wildlife, gardens, or parks____ Use binoculars, telescopes, microscopes, or magnifiers to____ Draw or photograph natural objects____

Source: Campbell 1997, 18.

Guided Discovery

Discovery learning is a concept introduced by Jerome Bruner in the 1960s. It is an approach where students work on their own to discover basic principles. Guided discovery is an adaptation of discovery learning where the teacher provides some direction. Unguided discovery is appropriate for preschool children, but in a typical elementary or secondary classroom, guided discovery is recommended. Unguided activities for older children usually prove unmanageable and unproductive. In guided discovery students are presented with intriguing questions, baffling situations, or interesting problems: *Why does the flame go out when we cover it with a jar? Why does this pencil seem to bend when you put it in water? What is the rule for grouping these words together?* Instead of explaining how to solve the problem, the teacher provides the appropriate materials and encourages students to make observations, form hypotheses, and test solutions. Feedback is given at the optimal moment, when students can either use it to revise their approach or take it as encouragement to continue in the direction they have chosen (Woolfolk 2001, 285).

The question has been raised: Is Discovery Learning Effective? Educators favoring discovery learning indicate that the approach is consistent with the ways that people learn and develop. It is reported that discovery learning matches cognitive development. Bruner identified three stages of cognitive growth that are similar to the stages identified by Piaget. According to Bruner, children move from an *enactive* stage to an *iconic* stage and finally to a *symbolic* stage.

In the enactive stage (similar to Piaget's sensorimotor stage), the child represents and understands the world through actions—to understand something is to manipulate it, taste it, throw it, break it, and so on. At the iconic stage, the child represents the world in images—appearances dominate. This stage corresponds to Piaget's preoperational thinking, in which the higher the water level, the more water there must be in the glass, because that's what appears to be true. At the final level, the child is able to use abstract ideas, symbols, language, and logic to understand and represent the world. Actions and images can still be used in thinking, but they do not dominate (Bruner 1966, 1971; Woolfolk 2001, 287).

Discovery learning allows students to move through these three stages as they encounter new information. First, students manipulate and act on materials; second, they form images as they note specific features and make observations; and, finally, they abstract general ideas and principles from these experiences and observations. Bruner believes students will have a better understanding of the topic because they have actually experienced each stage of representation. Many believe that when students are motivated and really participate in a discovery project, it leads to superior learning.

The Importance of Play

Much has already been discussed about the importance of play and its relationship to cognition in discussing the work and views of Jean Piaget (1962) and Lev Vygotsky (1978) earlier in this book. There is an increasing body of research on the connections between play on early learning and development; and, on cognitive competence.

In a comprehensive review of numerous studies on play, researchers provide evidence that play contributes to advances in "verbalization, vocabulary, language comprehension, attention span, imagination, concentration, impulse control, curiosity, problem-solving strategies, cooperation, empathy and group participation: (Smilansky & Shefatya 1990; Bodrova and Leong 2003). According to Bodrova and Leong (2003) recent research provides additional evidence of the strong connections between quality of play in pre-school years and children's readiness for school instruction (see Bowman, Donovan & Burns 2000; Shonkoff & Philips, 2000; Ewing Marion Kauffman Foundation, 2002). Further, research links play directly to children's ability to master academic content such as literacy and numeracy. Moreover, pretend play was found to be positively and significantly correlated with competencies as text comprehension, metalinguistic awareness and understanding of the purpose of reading and writing (Roskos & Christie 2000).

There is much in the research literature on the positive effects of *pretend play* in children's cognitive development. Bergen conducts an assessment of the literature on the topic and indicates that there is a growing body of evidence to suggest that high-quality pretend play is an important facilitator of cognitive competence.

Bergen (2002) cites many advantages of pretend play found from reviewing research studies:

- Pretend play requires the ability to transform objects and actions symbolically; it is furthered by interactive social dialogue and negotiation; and it involves role taking, script knowledge, and improvisation.
- Pretense plays a vital role in young children's lives and the period of its salience extends through the primary school years as well.
- It is likely that pretend play engages many areas of the brain because it involves emotion, cognition, language, and sensorimotor actions; and, thus, it may promote the development of dense synaptic connections (Bergen & Coscia 2001).
- High quality pretend and role play is an important facilitator of perspective taking and later abstract thought.

- Pretend play also promotes the development of private speech in play and in turn regulates behavior, eventually transforming private speech into self-regulation.
- Researchers suggest that social pretense, which requires children to determine task goals and carry them out, provides more opportunities for self-regulating private speech than do less complex play settings, and settings with tasks having predetermined goals and greater teacher direction.
- Kim (1999) compared 4- and 5- year-old children in conditions involving pretend play enactment of stories to conditions using storytelling. She found that children in the pretend play conditions used more elaborative narratives and had higher levels of narrative structure. Children also had better narrative recall immediately after the pretend enactment and at a later time period when prompted by pictures and doll figures.
- *Socio-dramatic play* has been shown effective in promoting problem-solving abilities (Fisher 1992). Other researchers found that there seems to be a reciprocal relationship between problem solving and pretend play, with *cooperative social play* having a more general influence on divergent problem solving and thematic play having a more specific influence on semantic problem solving (Wyver & Spence 1999).
- Research also has shown clear links between social and linguistic competence and high quality pretense; this leads to the conclusion that engagement in such pretense with peers may assist children's development in these areas.
- Numerous studies of literacy skill development through play, which embed literacy materials within play settings in preschool, kindergarten, and multiage programs, have typically shown increases in children's use of literacy materials and engagement in literacy acts (see, Christie & Enz 1992; Neuman & Roskos 1992; Stone & Christie 1996; and Einarsdottir 2000).

Play also is developmental, with children transitioning or advancing into what is known as *mature play*, which also corresponds to growth in cognitive dimensions. It is indicated that in the past, children learned how to play at a mature level simply by being part of an extended multi-age group within their own family or in their neighborhood. But unfortunately, with children today spending more time in age-segregated groups; and with TV and computers, this is no longer the case. The research documents the fact that TV shows and computers, even with carefully selected educational content, can not replace live play mentors. It is recommended that teachers take a primary role in helping children develop and maintain mature play. Research has found that teachers achieved the best results in terms of children's literacy development by supporting mature play. It is reported that children in classrooms where mature play was supported not only mastered literacy skills and concepts at a higher rate, but also developed better language and social skills and learned how to regulate their physical and cognitive behaviors (Bodrova, Leong, Norford, & Paynter, n.d.). By contrast, in the classrooms where play was on the back burner, teachers struggled with a variety of problems, including classroom management and children's lack of interest in reading and writing. These results suggest that thoughtful supported play is essential for young children's learning and development. This researcher would conclude that "structured" play, that is, carefully planned and designed play with end goals in mind, would be the appropriate instructional strategy. Table 4.3 outlines the characteristics of mature play based on research and best practices.

TABLE 4.3 Characteristics of Mature Play

Characteristics of Mature Play

IMAGINARY SITUATIONS	In mature play, children assign new meanings to the objects and people in a pretend situation. When children pretend, they focus on an object's abstract properties rather than its concrete attributes. They invent new uses for familiar toys and props when the play scenario calls for it. Sometimes children even describe the missing prop by using words and gestures, In doing so, they become aware of different symbolic systems that will serve them later when they start mastering letters and numbers.
MULTIPLE ROLES	The roles are not stereotypical or limited; the play easily includes supporting characters. When children assume different roles in play scenarios, they learn about real social interactions that they might not have experienced. They also learn their own actions and emotions by using them on demand. Understanding emotions and developing emotional self-control are crucial for children's social and emotional development.

CLEARLY DEFINED RULES	Mature play has clearly defined rules and roles. As children follow the rules in play, they learn to delay immediate fulfillment of their desires. Mature play helps young children develop self-regulation. To stay in the play the child must follow the rules.
FLEXIBLE THEMES	Mature play usually spans a broad range of themes that are flexible enough to incorporate new roles and ideas previously associated with other themes. When children play at a more mature level, they negotiate their plans. By combining different themes, children learn to plan and solve problems.
LANGUAGE DEVELOPMENT	A mature level of play implies an extensive use of language. Children use language to plan their play scenario, to negotiate and act out their roles, to explain their "pretend" behaviors to other participants, and to regulate compliance with the rules. In doing so, they often need to modify their speech (intonation, register, choice of words) according to the requirements of a particular role or as they switch from talking in a pretend way to talking for real. As the repertoire of roles grows, so do children's vocabulary, mastery of grammar and practical uses of language and metalinguistic awareness.
LENGTH OF PLAY	Mature play is not limited to one short session, but may last for many days as children pick up the theme where they left off and continue playing. Creating, reviewing, and revising the plans are essential parts of the play. Staying with the same play theme for a long time allows children to elaborate on the imaginary situation, integrate new roles, and discover new uses for play props.

Source: Bodrova & Leong 2003, 51.

The Concept of "Flow"

Mihaly Csikszentmihalyi (2005) has developed a concept known as "flow." Flow is a subjective state that people report when they are completely involved in something to the point of forgetting time, fatigue, and everything else but the activity itself. It is what we feel when we read a well-crafted novel, or play a good game of squash, or take part in a

stimulating conversation. The defining feature of flow is intense experiential involvement in moment-to-moment activity. Attention is fully invested in the task at hand, and the person functions at his or her fullest capacity.
According to Csikszentmihalyi,

> "Flow describes the spontaneous, effortless experience you achieve when you have a close match between a high level of challenge and the skills you need to meet the challenge. Flow happens when a person is completely involved in the task, is concentrating very deeply, and knows moment by moment what the next steps should be. If you're playing music, you know what note will come next, and you know how to play that note. You have a goal and you are getting feedback. The experience is almost addictive and very rewarding" (as told to Scherer 2002, 2).

It is reported that small children are in flow most of the time as they learn to walk and talk and other new things. They choose what to do and they match their skills with challenges. Unfortunately, they begin to lose this feeling once they go to school, according to Csikszentmihalyi, because they can not choose their goals and they can not choose the level at which they operate. They become increasingly passive.

When asked whether there were subjects or tasks that lend themselves to more engagement than others, it is reported that students get flow from group work, individual tasks, and quizzes, much more often than they do from listening to the teacher or from watching audiovisuals, according to Csikszentmihalyi (2005; Scherer 2002). Flow is easiest to experience when you are optimally challenged, have clear goals, and get clear immediate feedback.

Recommendations for teachers who want to structure instructional activities to achieve more flow or more engagement for students include the following:

- Show more relevance of what you are doing to the life of the student.
- Make clear the goal of every lesson.
- The student must know what he or she is supposed to achieve at the end.
- Teachers need a way to find out how well students are learning.
- Computer-assisted teaching can be useful because one can see their progress and change and correct their work as they progress.

Csikszentmihalyi believes that the optimal goal of education should be to allow students to explore their curiosity. He believes that no matter what a student is curious about, if they are really curious, they will have to learn everything else. Once the students are hooked on their interest, the teacher should be the gatekeeper to the enormous richness of information in the world. The role of the teacher is not to convey the same content to a captive audience. Further, Csikszentmihalyi says that

> "challenge gives children vision and direction, focus and perseverance. Support gives the serenity that allows them freedom from worry and fear...The important thing is to stimulate the curiosity, reinforce the curiosity, and build on the strengths of the child. And then you have a vibrant, lively community instead of people who have been stuffed with information that they don't care about" (2005; Scherer 2002, 15-16).

Differentiated Instruction

Another recommended strategy for teaching a diverse group of mixed-ability students is being able to differentiate or adapt instruction to meet their needs. A differentiated classroom offers a variety of learning options designed to tap into different readiness levels, interests, and learning profiles. In a differentiated class, the teacher uses a variety of ways for students to explore curriculum content; a variety of sense-making activities or processes through which students can come to understand and "own" information and ideas; and, a variety of options through which students can demonstrate or exhibit what they have learned (Tomlinson 1995; 2005). According to Tomlinson, four characteristics shape teaching and learning in an effective differentiated classroom:

- **Instruction is concept focused and principle driven.** All students have the opportunity to explore and apply the key concepts of the subject being studied. All students come to understand the key principles on which the study is based. Such instruction enables struggling learners to grasp and use powerful ideas and, at the same time, encourages advanced learners to expand their understanding and application of the key concepts and principles. Such instruction stresses understanding or sense-making rather than retention and regurgitation of fragmented bits of information. Concept-based and principle-driven instruction invites teachers to provide varied learning options. A "coverage-based" curriculum may cause a teacher to feel compelled to see that all students do the same work. In the former, all students have the opportunity to explore meaningful ideas through a variety of avenues and approaches.
- **On-going assessment of student readiness and growth are built into the curriculum.** Teachers do not assume that all students need a given task or segment of study, but continuously assess student readiness and interest, providing support when students need additional instruction

and guidance, and extending student exploration when indications are that a student or group of students is ready to move ahead.
- **Flexible grouping is consistently used.** In a differentiated class, students work in many patterns. Sometimes they work alone, sometimes in pairs, sometimes in groups. Sometimes tasks are readiness-based, sometimes interest-based, sometimes constructed to match learning style, and sometimes a combination of readiness, interests, and learning style. In a differentiated classroom, whole-group instruction may also be used for introducing new ideas, when planning, and for sharing learning outcomes.

- **Students are active explorers.** Teachers guide the exploration. Because varied activities often occur simultaneously in a differentiated classroom, the teacher works more as a guide or facilitator of learning than as a dispenser of information. As in a large family, students must learn to be responsible for their own work. Not only does such student-centeredness give students more ownership of their learning, but it also facilitates the important goal of growing independence in thought, planning and evaluation. Implicit in such instruction is 1) goal setting shared by teacher and student based on student readiness, interest, and learning profile, and 2) assessment predicated on student growth and goal attainment.
(Tomlinson 1995)

Role of Technology

A major question relative to the topic of enriching children's lives is: how can technology stimulate children's thinking and development? Although television, cameras, videos, fax machines and portable keyboards are considered technology, this research focuses on the use of computers and similar innovative artificial intelligence, including robotics.

The current research literature is divided on this topic. The division parallels the discussion on traditional versus innovative teaching methodologies in the classroom. The largest study against the use of computers in children's learning cites the serious health hazards to children, including repetitive stress injuries, eyestrain, obesity, social isolation, and, for some, long-term physical, emotional or intellectual developmental damage (Cordes and Miller 2000; see also Healy 1998). Further, these critics are concerned that computer use will inhibit language development and lead to social isolation. But, further examination of the research reveals many positive findings and much discussion about the positive benefits of the use of technology in children's development, including experimental models that are being tested; and an assessment of their impact on learning and the developmental domains.

In a report by the Northwest Regional Educational Laboratory on Technology in Early Childhood Education (Scoter, Ellis & Railsback 2001) the following questions were examined:
- What are appropriate and meaningful uses of technology with children?
- How can educators take advantage of the power of these tools to enhance children's learning and development, while avoiding potential problems?

The research report provides a detailed analysis of related studies on the subject and study questions. Two key conclusions of the report are as follows:
- *New interactive technologies make it easier to create environments in which students can learn by doing; and,*
- *Technologies can help people visualize difficult-to-understand concepts* (6).

Further, examples are provided of the types of uses early childhood experts recommend as being developmentally appropriate and allow children to create and explore. They include the following delineation:
- *Software that allows children to compose and record music using synthesizers;*
- *Write programs that draw mathematical shapes on the screen and use on-screen manipulatives to deepen mathematical understanding;*
- *Talking word processing software that provides immediate spoken feedback on letter names and letter combinations to novice reader/writers as they experiment with written language* (Scoter et al. 4)

In reviewing the literature, the report also indicates that there is a large body of research highlighting the use of technology on the enhancement of social and emotional, language, motor development and physical well-being and cognitive skills. Table 4.4 describes the key research findings of the impact of technology on children's development by the specific domains.

TABLE 4.4 Impact of Technology on Children's Social, Emotional, Language, Physical, Motor and Cognitive Development

DEVELOPMENTAL DOMAIN	POTENTIAL IMPACT
Social and Emotional Development	• Computers and software can serve as catalysts for social interaction and conversations. Such use will increase and not impair language and literacy development. Strategies to build such socialization includes having students pair up at computers, placing computers in close proximity so students can share ideas or locating computers in a central spot that would invite other children to participate (Clements & Nastasi 1993;Clements 1999). [This could now be resolved with the use of projectors and screens where computer pages could be projected on a larger screen.] • Computers are intrinsically motivating for young children, and contribute to cognitive and social development (National Association for the Education of Young Children (NAEYC) 1996). • Computers can enhance children's self-concept and improve their attitudes about learning (Sivin-Kachala & Bialo 1994).
Language Development	• The variety of rich experiences that promote early literacy, including conversations with caring adults, storytelling, drawing and painting, and pretend play, is critical in the development of both oral and written language (Novick 1998).

	• Technology has a place in this environment; language and literacy development are major strengths of technology use with young children through the opportunities and motivation it provides.
	• Computer play encourages longer, more complex speech and the development of fluency (Davidson & Wright 1994).
	• Children tend to narrate what they are doing as they draw pictures or move objects and characters around on the screen (Bredekamp & Rosegrant 1994).
	• Young children interacting at computers engage in high levels of spoken communication and cooperation, such as turn-taking and peer collaboration. "Compared to more traditional activities, such as puzzle assembly or block building, the computer elicits more social interaction and different types of interaction" (Clements, Nastasi, & Swaminathan 1993, 60).
Physical Well-Being and Motor Development	• Fine and gross motor skills develop at varying rates, and learning to write can be tedious and difficult as children struggle to form letters. A word processor allows them to compose and revise text without being distracted by the fine motor aspects of letter formation (Davis & Shade 1994).
	• Following ergonomic standards would be important to prevent muscular-skeletal injuries and vision problems. Computer use

	is and should be relatively brief at this age, with limited screen time and frequent breaks.
	• Lack of exercise and obesity are serious problems that should be addressed. Children two to seven years old spend an average of 11 minutes using a computer, but more than 3 hours watching television and videos (Roberts, Foehr, Rideout, & Brodie 1999). Screen time (including TV, computer, and video games) should be limited to a maximum of one to two hours per day for young children (American Academy of Pediatrics 2000; Healy 1999). Vigorous physical activities and play should be encouraged.
COGNITION AND GENERAL KNOWLEDGE	• Technology offers unique intellectual experiences and opportunities for young children. Computers allow representation and actions not possible in the physical world. Children can manipulate variables such as gravity and speed, and discover the resulting effects (Clements 1999; Seng 1998).
	• There are positive effects of technology use on cognitive and social learning and development (Clements 1994; Haugland & Shade 1994). In similar studies with different ages of children, computer use along with supporting activities (e.g., manipulatives, objects used to understand concepts) provided greater benefits than either one alone.
	• Compared to children in a similar classroom without

- computer use or experience, three- and four- year-olds who used computers with supporting activities had significantly greater gains in verbal and nonverbal skills, problem-solving, abstraction, and conceptual skills (Haugland 1992).

- Third-grade children who used both manipulatives and computer programs showed more sophistication in classification and logical thinking than children who used only manipulatives (Clements & Natasi 1993).

- Technology use should be connected to what children already know and can build upon. This leads to greater motivation and self-direction.

- Open-ended software—provides opportunities to discover make choices and find out the impact of decisions. It also encourages exploration, imagination, and problem-solving; as opposed to drill-and-practice software that inhibits creativity.

Source: Scoter, Ellis & Railsback 2001.

Relative to computer use by age, the Northwest Regional Education Laboratory report indicates that computer use for most children under the age of three years does not have meaning for the child. For ages 3 to 5 years or preschool age, learning through exploration and discovery is crucial; therefore, the value of the computer is in its open-ended use, and not in creating a product. The teacher's role is to create an environment in which children become aware and explore, and then act to support their exploration and inquiry in many different ways. For children 5 to 8 years of age, increased opportunities for independent use should become available as there is increasing language and literacy skills development. For example, it is indicated that simple word processors become important educational tools as children experiment with written language. The teacher's role is to be less involved in directing the activities and more involved in monitoring activities, by intervening as necessary to guide and pose questions that encourage thinking (Scoter et al. 2001).

Relative to computer use and its contribution to the development of children's writing, it is reported that written language, like oral language, is learned by doing things with words in the real world using language for a purpose. Early childhood classrooms encourage written literacy by providing materials to use in pretend play, and by encouraging children to express themselves in writing. Studies indicate that word-processing software encourages writing, and leads to increased motivation and improvement in writing skills. Computers and writing programs can be used with preschool-aged children to explore written language, and their use can be successfully integrated into process-oriented writing programs as early as first grade or kindergarten. It is reported that such software does the following:

- Provides critical support, or scaffolding, for young writers, enabling them to perform tasks they could not perform by themselves (Clements & Nastasi 1993).
- Allows children to compose longer and more complex stories and worry less about mistakes (Davis & Shade 1994).
- Facilitates positive attitudes toward writing and word processing among children from kindergarten through primary grades (Clements & Nastasi 1993).
- Encourages students to write more, more effectively, and with greater fluency (Apple Classrooms of Tomorrow 1995).
- Helps children gain confidence in their writing and increases motivation to write more when using computers than with paper and pencil (Clements & Natasi 1993).

Impact of Computer-Based Technologies

In a report on the impact of technology on children's learning, Roschelle and others (2000), conclude from their research that computer technology can help support learning and is especially useful in developing the higher order skills of critical thinking, analysis, and scientific inquiry. Further, they indicate that technology enhances four characteristics of learning: 1) active engagement, 2) participation in groups, 3) frequent interaction and feedback, and 4) connections to real-world contexts. Table 4.5 is a listing of the findings on the four characteristics of learning enhanced by use of technology.

TABLE4.5 Impact of technology on four characteristics of learning

CHARACTERISTICS OF LEARNING	RESEARCH FINDINGS
Learning Through Active Engagement	Using technology to engage students more actively in learning is not limited to science and mathematics. Computer-based applications such as desk-top publishing and desktop video can be used to involve students more actively in constructing presentations that reflect students' understanding and knowledge of various subjects. Although previous media technologies generally placed children in the role of passive observers, these new technologies make content construction much more accessible to students, and research indicates that such uses of technology can have significant positive effects. In one project, inner-city high school students worked as 'multimedia designers' to create an electronic school yearbook and displays for a local children's museum. The students participating in the project showed significant gains in task engagement and self-confidence measures compared with students enrolled in a more traditional computer class.
Learning Through Participation in Groups	Reports from researchers and teachers suggest that students who participate in computer-connected learning networks show increased motivation, a deeper understanding of concepts, and an increased willingness to tackle difficult questions. In one collaborative technology project, Computer Supported Intentional Learning Environment (CSILE), the goal is to support structured collaborative knowledge building by having students communicate their ideas and criticisms—in the form of questions, statement, and diagrams—to a shared database classified by different types of thinking. In this project, students become more aware of how to organize their knowledge. It also permits students to participate

	independent of their physical location. Students work with students in schools and classrooms from around the globe to build a common understanding of a problem or topic. The impact of this program has been that students perform better on standardized tests and create deeper explanations than students in classes without technology.
Learning Through Frequent Interaction and Feedback	Research suggests that learning proceeds most rapidly when learners have frequent opportunities to apply the ideas they are learning and when feedback on the success or failure of an idea comes almost immediately.
	Computer technology supports this learning principle in 3 ways: 1)computer tools can encourage rapid interaction and feedback—for example, using interactive graphing, a student may explore the behavior of a mathematical model very rapidly, getting a quicker feel for the range of variation in the model; 2) computer tools can engage students for extended periods on their own or in small groups; this can create more time for the teacher to give individual feedback to particular children; and, 3) computer tools can be used to analyze each child's performance and provide more timely and targeted feedback than the student typically receives.
Learning Through Connections to Real-World Contexts	Computer technology can provide students with an excellent tool for applying concepts in a variety of contexts, thereby breaking the artificial isolation of school subject matter from real-world situations.
	For example, through the communication features of computer-based technology, students have access to the latest scientific data and expeditions, whether from a National Air and Space Administration's (NASA) mission to Mars, an ongoing archeological dig in Mexico, or a remotely controlled telescope in Hawaii. Further, technology can bring unprecedented opportunities for students

> to actively participate in the kind of experimentation, design, and reflection that professionals routinely do, with access to the same tools professionals use.
>
> Through the Internet, students from around the world can work as partners to scientists, business-people, and policymakers who are making valuable contributions to society.
>
> One important project that allows students to actively participate in a real-world research project is the Global Learning and Observations to Benefit the Environment (GLOBE) Program, developed in 1992 by Vice President Al Gore, as an innovative way to aid the environment and help students learn science. The GLOBE Program links more than 3,800 schools around the world to scientists. (See more about this program in the Models chapter.)

Source: Roschelle, Pea, Hoadley, Gordin, and Means 2000.

Computer-based technology can also improve what children learn by providing exposure to ideas and experiences that would be inaccessible for most children any other way. Examples include the following:
- Because synthesizers can make music, students can experiment with composing music even before they can play an instrument.
- Because communications technology makes it possible to see and talk to others in different parts of the world, students can learn about archeology by following the progress of a real dig in the jungles of Mexico.
- Through online communications, students can reach beyond their own community to find teachers and other students who share their academic interests.
- By using the computers' capacity for simulation, dynamically linked notations, and interactivity, ordinary students can achieve extraordinary command of sophisticated concepts (Roschelle et al. 2000).

According to the research, computer-based applications also have had significant effects on what children learn in specific subject areas. Table 4.6 is a summary overview of select computer-based applications or programs and their impact on what children have learned in the areas of science, mathematics and the humanities.

Roschelle et al., also provides an overview of select program models illustrating the effects of computer-based technologies. These will be presented, along with other interesting models found, in the next chapter on selected models.

TABLE 4.6 Summary of select disciplines using computer-based technology.

Subject/Discipline	Findings
Science: Visualization, Modeling and Simulation	Computer-based applications using visualization, modeling, and simulation have proven to be powerful tools for teaching scientific concepts. The research literature abounds with successful applications that have enabled students to master concepts usually considered too sophisticated for their grade level. Examples include technology using dynamic diagram such as pictures that can move in response to a range of input which can help students visualize and understand the forces underlying various phenomena. Involving students in making sense of computer simulations that model physical phenomena, but defy intuitive explanations, also has been shown to be a useful technique. One example of this work is ThinkerTools, a simulation program that allows middle school students to visualize the concepts of velocity and acceleration. (See Models in next chapter.)
Mathematics: Dynamic, Linked Notations	Researchers have found that the move from traditional paper-based mathematical notations to onscreen notions including algebraic symbols, graphs, tables and geometric figures) can have a dramatic effect. In comparison to paper and pencil which supports only static, isolated notations, use of computers allows for "dynamic linked notations" with several helpful advantages: -Students can explore changes rapidly in the notation by dragging with a mouse, as opposed to slowly rewriting the changes. -Students can see the effects of changing one notation on another, such as modifying the value of a parameter of an equation and seeing how the resulting graph changes its shape.

	-Students can receive feedback when they create a notation that is incorrect. For example a computer can beef if a student tries to sketch a nonsensical mathematical function in a graph. An example is the SimCalc Project which has shown that computers can help middle school students in some of the most challenging urban settings to learn calculus concepts such as rate, accumulation, limit, and mean value. (See models.)
Social Studies, Language and the Arts	The commercially successful SimCity game (an interactive simulation rather than a traditional video game) has been used to teach students about urban planning.
	Computer-based tools have been designed to allow students to choreograph a scene in a Shakespeare play or to explore classic movies, such as Citizen Kane, from multiple points of view to increase their ability to consider alternative literary interpretations.
	The Perseus Project provides students with access to a pioneering multimedia learning environment for exploring hyperlinked documents and cultural artifacts from ancient civilizations. Similar software can provide interactive media environments for classes in the arts.
	One recent study documented the experience of two sixth-grade classes participating in a social studies project on the Spanish colonization of Latin America. The study found that students who used computers to create a multimedia presentation on what they learned scored significantly higher on a posttest as compared to students of the other sixth grade class that completed a textbook-based unit on the same topic.
	In a study examining effectiveness of using interactive storybooks to develop basic language skills found that first graders using a technology-based system demonstrated significantly greater gains compared to those receiving traditional instruction.
	Elementary and middle school children alternate between playing musical instruments, singing, and programming music on the computer using Tuneblocks, a musical version of the Logo programming language. Case studies show how using the software enables ordinary children to learn abstract musical concepts like phrase, figure, and meter—concepts taught in college music theory classes.

Innovative and Futuristic Technologies

Two studies were found that speculated on the future possibilities of technology that could deepen student learning. Mitchel Resnick at the MIT Media Laboratory sees the future potential of computers. He believes that computers will not live up to their full potential until people start thinking about them more like finger paint and less like television. With finger paint, unlike television, people can create their own pictures. Computers can be used in a similar way, according to Resnick.

> "In addition to accessing Web pages, people can create their own web pages. In addition to downloading MP3 music files, people can create their own music compositions. In addition to playing SimCity, people can create their own simulated worlds. These types of activities are especially important in the lives of children" (Resnick 2000, 174).

He indicates that research has shown that many of children's best learning experiences come when they are engaged in designing and creating things, especially things that are meaningful to themselves and others around them. He states further:

> "Computers, like finger paint, blocks, and beads, can be used as a "material" for making things. Compared with traditional materials, computers expand the range of things that children can create—and the range of concepts that they can learn while creating. But in most places today, computers aren't used in this way....children most often use computers for playing games or accessing information on the Web. Only rarely do they use computers to create, to design, or to invent" (174).

Resnick believes that too many people view education as a process of transmitting information from teacher to learner, rather than as a process in which learners actively build an understanding of the world based on their experiences and interactions. Very seldom do people look for new ways for children to create, experiment, or explore; but rather they look for new ways to transmit information.

For Resnick, an important challenge for the future is to develop a new generation of computer technologies worthy of this new generation of children. Ideally, these new technologies should provide children with "design leverage," enabling them to learn concepts that would have been difficult for them to learn in the past. Based on this futuristic perspective, Resnick and his research team at the MIT Media Laboratory has developed and is piloting a family of "programmable bricks:" tiny computers embedded inside children's building blocks. With these bricks, children can build computational power directly into their physical world constructions, blurring the boundaries between the physical and digital worlds.

Resnick reports that in pilot studies, children have used programmable bricks to build a variety of creative constructions, including an odometer for roller blades (using a magnetic sensor to count wheel rotations), a diary security system (using a touch sensor to detect if anyone tried to open the diary), and an automated hamster cage (using a light sensor to monitor the hamster's movements during the day).

Resnick cites one particular learning experience of an 11-year-old girl named Jenny. She was interested in birds and decided to use programmable bricks to build a new type of bird feeder. She started by making a wooden lever that served as a perch for the birds. When a bird landed, it would trigger a touch sensor, sending a signal to a programmable brick, which turned on a Lego mechanism, which then pushed down the shutter of a camera, taking a picture of the bird. Resnick believes the project served as a rich context for engaging in scientific inquiry and learning science-related concepts.

Further, Jenny developed a deeper understanding of certain concepts she had previously studied in school, but never fully appreciated. She also began to work with engineering concepts that have traditionally been taught at the university level only.

Resnick believes that helping all children become truly fluent with computer technologies will require new types of technology, new educational strategies, and new public policies; and, a new public understanding of the nature of learning. *"It is the only way that computers will have a deep and lasting impact on the lives of children,"* according to Resnick.

Mary Burns, a senior technology specialist at the Education Development Center in Massachusetts, poses a critical question:

- *Why are schools using computers primarily to teach low level skills when technology has the potential to deepen student learning?* (2006).

She believes that computers can provide transformative student learning experiences that would otherwise not be possible. But she also believes that educators need to be asking critical questions about what students are really learning. She asserts that students in classrooms generally use lower-order applications that offer few opportunities for problem-solving, analysis, and evaluation. She states further:

"In addition to lower-order tools, classrooms use more robust tools, such as the Internet, in such nondifferentiated ways that they dilute their power.

Although students use the Internet to access information, I have seen little evidence of students engaging in more complex and dynamic kinds of online learning opportunities, such as online collaboration or content-oriented simulations—despite the fact that much of the rationale for broadband access in schools was for students to take part in such opportunities. Instead, students generally use the Internet as an electronic textbook, often without questioning, validating, or evaluating the information they find."(50).

Burns believes that a great deal of Internet use by students is intellectually passive, with the greatest amount of activity occurring at the fine motor level—pointing, clicking, and copying and pasting large amounts of text into Microsoft Word, PowerPoint or Publisher. In fact she recommends more developmentally appropriate and challenging tools be emphasized, such as, spreadsheets and databases that can offer richer opportunities to practice analytical and critical thinking skills.

It is a prevailing view that teachers and students must become creators of information and ideas; and, not simply users of technology. Therefore, it is recommended that the instructional technology community focus on the role of computers as learning tools. The instructional technology community needs to actively encourage teachers to reflect on technology and engage them in discussions about technology's role in fostering learning. Burns poses some reflective questions for teachers to ponder:
- What kinds of software should I use in the classroom, and why?
- When should my students use computers in class? When should they not use them?
- Does the current technology use in my classroom support the curriculum and deepen content? How?
- Do certain uses of technology match certain learning outcomes?
- Does my current technology use improve my students' learning? (Burns 2006, 52).

These and other reflective questions could be transformational in changing the existing paradigm of instructional technology into a more realistic and meaningful model that truly deepens learning and provides meaningful and stimulating experiences for students.

PART FIVE

SELECTED INNOVATIVE MODELS

Overview

In addition to examining the research literature and studies on alternatives to traditional modes of teaching and learning, this author also began to search for examples of program models, instructional strategies and technology applications found to be stimulating, exciting and motivating for students. Further, models were selected where implementers believed their strategies had a positive effect on student learning in the developmental domains; or, where results were empirically tested for their effectiveness. Other criteria for selection of programs included the following:

- Programs, models or strategies that were student-, learning-, or subject-focused.
- Programs, models or strategies that were well defined and solely developed or designed to stimulate children's learning and development.
- Programs and models using innovative or novel designs or strategies.
- Programs, models or strategies addressing one or all of the developmental domains.
- Programs, models or strategies allowing for student independence, flexibility and the ability to construct and reconstruct knowledge and meaning.
- Programs, models or strategies that were stimulating and motivating.
- Programs, models or strategies that were structured but left room for student input and collaboration.
- Programs, models or strategies addressing assessment of outcomes or impact on student learning.

The selected programs, models or strategies have been classified into categories, with some overlap where one program may fall into several

categories. In examining the particular programs and their thrust, the following categories emerged:
- School Programs;
- Unique Teaching and Learning Strategies for the Classroom;
- Use of Multiple Intelligences;
- Inquiry and Problem-Based Learning;
- Unique Science Projects;
- Service and Other Field-Based Learning;
- Innovative Instructional Technology; and,
- Globalization Projects.

Table 5.1 is a listing of programs found by the above categories. Tables 5.2 through 5.9 is a more detailed description of the teaching and learning features of each model, along with target and type of students served, program components and reported outcomes.

Enriching the Lives of Children

TABLE 5.1 Overview of Select Innovative Programs, Models and Strategies by Category

Programs	Strategies	MI Theory	Inquiry/Problem	Science	Service/Field	Technology	Global
British Infant Schools	Bibliotherapy	Virginia Think Tank	Inquiring Scientists	Inquiring Scientists	Campus Calgary	MIT- Programmable Bricks	Global Educ.
The Eureka Model	Celebrity Interviews	Key Learning Community	Enrichment Clusters	Science Beyond the Class-Room		Micro-Computer Lab in Creek Biology	Travel Schooling
Key Learning Community	Science Beyond the Classroom	Brain-Flex Project, New South Wales	The River City MUVE Project (Multi-User Virtual Environment Experiential Simulator)	The River City MUVE Project		Computer-Supported Intentional Learning Environment (CSILE Project)	World Lit.
Character Education Partnership	Early Arts Education	Project Spectrum				GLOBE- The Global Learning and Observations to Benefit the Environment Program	Global Education Program- Jordan

Programs	Strategies	MI Theory	Inquiry/Problem	Science	Service/Field	Technology	Global
GLOBE- The Global Learning and Observations to Benefit the Environment Program	Higher Order Thinking Skills Project (H.O.T.S.)	New Canaan Summer Camp				ThinkerTools	WorldQuest
Reggio Emilia-Italy	Civic Virtues-Political Education	Australia Public Schools				SimCalc	
	Chess Clubs Roberto Clemente Middle School	Reggio Emilia-Italy				Digital Storytelling-Juneau, Alaska	
						The GenYES Mentoring Model	
						Robotic Pets	

Enriching the Lives of Children

Programs	Strategies	MI Theory	Inquiry/Problem	Science	Service/Field	Technology	Global
						The River City MUVE Project	

TABLE 5.2 Selected Large-Scale Programs (Several Schools, District or Statewide, National or International)

BRITISH INFANT SCHOOLS, ENGLAND

Target Grade(s) or Age(s): 5,6,7 years

Program Treatment: Open Education. Classes family grouped; children of 2 or 3 different ages in same classes. No class periods. Integrated day.

Many subjects taught or activities held at same time. Children work individually or in small groups; teacher seldom lectures; teacher weaves in and out of groups helping children learn in their own fashion.

Class may be organized into interest centers and organized for independent use. Centers represent interest of teachers and students.

Active learning. Subjects taught in inquiring manner. Play is key to learning.
Learning takes place as a result of expression. Children encouraged in writing, painting, drawing, acting, or dancing— modes of expression used to move child's level of understanding forward.

Children often in role of teacher as aid to their own understanding.

Assessment & Reported Outcomes: None reported.

Comments: More information is needed on this model, as well as information on student outcomes.

THE EUREKA MODEL
(Szold Institute for Research in the Behavioral Sciences), Israel

Initially implemented in 2 schools in Tel-Aviv. Currently nationwide in 56 schools in the Arab, Bedouin and Druze sectors, and in the Jewish sector, where the focus is on schools catering to students from lower socio-economic backgrounds, and new immigrants from Ethiopia and the Russian Republics. Program focuses on visual arts and sciences. See Zorman, 1997.

Target Grade(s) or Age(s): Elementary School Children from different socio-economic and cultural backgrounds.

Program Treatment: A cross-cultural model for identifying gifted and hidden talents among children from different socio-economic and cultural backgrounds. The program is based on providing students with enrichment experiences related to their culture and environment and the children's behaviors are observed and recorded. Products are also collected and evaluated. Has 2 program phases: Exposure and Immersion.

Phase 1: Exposure: Hands on experiences in talent areas for first 2 years of school, with observations and evaluation of work. Learning environments are designed around themes and concepts in line with the students' and teachers' culture, environment, needs and relevancy to student's lives.

Examples of curriculum:
1st graders being taught about seasons and changes that occur. Students living close to the sea explore and observe the sea in different seasons, including the animals, colors of the sea, and changes during different times of the day and so on. They paint pictures of the sea, listen to stories and tell stories of their own about the sea.
Student living in the mountains of Jerusalem, focus on seasonal changes in different landscapes. Comparisons and contrasts are made and how different weather factors affect them during the seasons. Students create a diorama of the different landscapes, using concepts such as perspective and include features of the landscapes, e.g., houses, crops, people, etc.

In the desert region near Be'er-Sheba, teachers focus on the cycle of growth of seeds. Students collect seeds from trees and other environments. They draw, paint, dissect, examine, and conduct controlled experiments with seeds in school and at home. They learn about conditions needed for growth and learn about experimental replication. They discuss the concept of cycles—of growth of plants to the cycle of the seasons. They form analogies to the cycle of human development. The compare and contrast the growth of a seed to a developing embryo. They convey and depict meaning and significance in drawings and paintings.

Phase 2: Immersion (3rd grade and up).

Students who are identified as talented explore in-depth their talent areas in special programs. Every school district that adapts the model decides which type of special program caters best to its students' needs. Students are exposed to enrichment days in a neighborhood school, enrichment courses at the end of the school day, and enrichment courses provided by a regional center, a college or a museum in the afternoon.

Students not identified as talented, continue to be exposed to various content areas as part of their school curriculum, in a manner similar to the phase of exposure. At the end of the school year, students whose performance and motivation improves based on assessment join the special programs.

Examples of instructional program: For sixth grades the study of architecture, which culminates in an individual project. Students construct a model of their dream house. Students must search for resource books on various schools or architecture at different time periods. They learn about physical principles in house design, and study how the principles are expressed in works of art in exhibits, slides and books. They experiment with principles by building models of architectural structures.

They also design their own dream house and build a model of it. Models designed by children include a boat house, a theater modeled after Shakespeare's globe, a café, and models of suburban and town houses.

Assessment & Reported Outcomes: Assessment:
-Teacher ratings of students' behavior.
-Professional evaluation of portfolios.
-Task performance.

Program was a seven-year longitudinal study. Assessment included teachers, parents and students.

Program was found to have a very high appeal to students. Program participation encourages students to continue to pursue their fields of talent on a more advanced level.

Comments: Impacts all developmental domains, with great emphasis on creativity.

Enriching the Lives of Children

THE KEY LEARNING COMMUNITY
Indianapolis, Indiana
Website: http://www.616.ips.k12.in.us

Target Grade(s) or Age(s): K-12

Program Treatment: A multiple intelligences school based on Howard Gardner's theory. They value learning and look for student's strengths in each of the eight intelligences. Students explore and study all eight intelligences during the regular school day.

The school values intrinsic motivation. They work to help students find interest and meaning in their daily work through multi-age, multi-ability groups in a project-based environment. Classes such as Flow and Pod help student explore their own interests and build strengths. Each day, students can focus on activities that highlight intelligences and combinations of intelligences that they favor.

The school curriculum features periodic themes (such as Mexico, the "rebirth" of Indianapolis, patterns, birds); working alone or in small groups, students create their own projects, inspired by the theme. The completed projects are presented to classmates, described and critiqued, and the whole activity is videotaped. Projects serve as an excellent showcase for a child's interests, themes, and configuration of intelligences.

Assessment & Reported Outcomes: The school has developed an extensive set of performance criteria that students must meet at each level. They have designed an authentic assessment system.

At the elementary and middle school level, the school assesses student progress based on levels of achievement within performance descriptors. Student motivation also is assessed including whether the student is intrinsic, extrinsic, passive or disruptive.

High school students are required to complete an apprenticeship in their area of strength as a prerequisite to graduation. Further, students must document, in a profile multimedia portfolio (with sound, graphics and text), their participation and applied knowledge regarding eight human commonalities as identified by Ernest Boyer. *Visit website to download extensive assessment criteria in PDF.*

Comments: The Key School was one of the first institutions to pilot Gardner's MI theory. They originally began as a K-6 program in 1987, with 150 students. Grades 7-8 were added in 1993. Now they have expanded to grades 9 to 12, with the first graduating class in 2003. Impacts all developmental domains; with great emphasis on creativity.

THE CHARACTER EDUCATION PARTNERSHIP (National)
Website: http://www.cortland.edu/character

Target Grade(s) or Age(s): K-12

Program Treatment: The program seeks to develop virtue and human excellence. The program takes deliberate steps to cultivate moral and intellectual virtues through every phase of school life—the example of adults, the relationships among peers, the handling of discipline, the resolution of conflict, the content of the curriculum, the process of instruction, the rigor of academic standards, the environment of the school, the conduct of extracurricular activities, and the involvement of parents.

Students are taught character through the curriculum by example, case studies and scenarios. Students are also taught the skills of mediation and conflict resolution. Students have the opportunity for ethical reflection, the teaching of character through the curriculum, learning how to develop a democratic classroom and more.

The program also encompasses the cognitive, affective and behavioral domains. The cognitive domain includes, perspective-taking, moral reasoning, thoughtful decision making, and moral self- knowledge. The program also addresses the development of competence, will and moral habit.

Other strategies include cooperative learning, moral reflection through reading, research, essay writing, journal keeping, discussion and debate.

Assessment & Reported Outcomes: *The program has a variety of assessment instruments for evaluating the program in totality and its various components. The website includes a primer for evaluating character education programs Character Education Quality Standards outlines key components of effective character education and allows schools and districts to evaluate their efforts in relation to these criteria. This instrument provides a means for educators, administrators, and community members to reflect on current practices, identify short- and long-term objectives, and develop or improve a strategic plan.*

Character Education Quality Standards is based on CEP's Eleven Principles of Effective Character Education™ and the Eleven Principles Survey by Tom Lickona and Matthew Davidson.

Enriching the Lives of Children

Twelve Component Assessment and Planning (TCAP) Davidson, Lickona, and Khmelkov (2004), is a planning and assessment tool constructed for use with the s 12-Point Comprehensive Approach to Character Education. The instrument provides outcome indicators for each component of the comprehensive approach. It may be used in its entirety or one component at a time. Additional space is provided for supplemental items measure outcome indicators specific to particular program contexts.

Comments: A program for development of moral character, but also impacts cognitive and social and emotional development.

GLOBE
(Global Learning and Observations to Benefit the Environment Program)
An international program.
Website: www.globe.gov

Target Grade(s) or Age(s): K-12

Program Treatment: A hands-on education and science program. Teachers and students collect local environmental data for use by scientists, and the scientists provide mentoring to the teachers and students about how to apply scientific concepts in analyzing real environmental problems. The program depends on students to help monitor the environment while educating them about it.

Assessment & Reported Outcomes: Students are more motivated to become more engaged in learning because they are making a difference by aiding real scientific research. Thus, their data collection ahs real value.

In a 1998 survey, 62% of teachers using the GLOBE Program reported that they had students analyze, discuss, or interpret the data. GLOBE teachers said they view the program as very effective and indicated that the greatest student gains occurred in the areas of observational and measurement skills, ability to work in small groups and technology/skills.

Comments: Begun in 1992 by Vice President Al Gore as an innovative way to aid the environment and help students learn science. The GLOBE program links more than 3,800 schools around the world to scientists. Impacts all developmental domains.

REGGIO EMILIA, ITALY-APPROACH TO PRESCHOOL EDUCATION
Twenty-two municipal preschools and thirteen infant and toddler day care centers.

Target Grade(s) or Age(s): Schools for infants from under 1 year to three years. Schools for preschoolers, three to six years.

Program Treatment: Buildings are beautiful and spacious—ample, open, streaming with light, potted plants, inviting chairs and couches (Gardner 1999).
School has been fashioned that best suits the entire community: teachers, parents, the physical setting, the region and the children.

Type and quality of activities for children are different. In each class, groups of children spend several months exploring a theme of interest. Themes attract young children because they offer rich sensory stimulation and raise intriguing puzzles.
Most projects center on aspects of the natural world—plants, animals, and objects (such as stones) and events (such as rainstorms) that easily arouse children's interest, perceptions and feelings. Projects also include human artifacts.
Examples include sunlight, rainbows, raindrops, shadows, the city, a city for ants, the town lions, poppy fields, amusement park for birds, operation of the fax machine and more.

Children approach objects, themes, and environments from many angles; they ponder questions and phenomena during explorations. They end up creating artful objects that capture their interests and their learning: drawings, paintings, cartoons, charts, photographic series, toy models, replicas and more.

Objects and products created are placed on display for parents and the community to learn from them. Many of these theme-inspired artifacts have made their way into books, traveling exhibitions and wall displays in their own and other schools. Many of the children's works are reported to be substantial and evocative creations.

Activities for the next day or next week grow out of the results, problems, and puzzles of the current week; the cycle is repeated so long as it proves fruitful. Children and teachers are continually reflecting on the meaning of an activity, which issues it raises, and how its depths and range can be productively probed.

Enriching the Lives of Children

Teachers also act on natural environment for instruction. For example, when a rainbow appears or there is rain, or if it is cloudy. Children set up observation posts and confer on the reasons why and consider how to better prepare for the next sighting of a rainbow. In the following weeks children read and write stories about rainbows, explore raindrops, consider rainbow like phenomena that accompany lawn hoses and mist, etc.

Assessment & Reported Outcomes: In the early 1990s, Newsweek declared the preschools of Reggio were the best in the world.

Teachers spend much time documenting student work. Techniques are continually improved. Teachers carefully document discussions, particular actions, drafts, and works of children. Teachers develop elaborate systems for recording individual and collective activities and progress of children for anyone to review. They use audiotapes, videotapes, still photographs and paper and pen. It is reported that teachers document so much that children model the behavior as they observe phenomena.

A goal of assessment is to document, capture and make public the hundreds of languages—some oral, some bodily, some artistic—that children naturally use, produce and share with one another. Much interaction and exchange takes place between teachers, students, parents and members of the community.

Gardner's assessment of Reggio programs (1999):

"Reggio encourages the cultivation and elaboration of multiple representations, multiple intelligences…and furnishes a powerful set of entry points to the community's cherished truths, sense of beauty, and ethical standards. The Reggio approach invites children to explore, in multiple, comfortable ways, the physical materials with which to capture one's impressions; it shares the insights with the rest of the community; and it models a set of respectful human relations that should extend throughout the life cycle" (91).

It is reported that staff have shown little interest in documenting for the public what children are learning in a more formal or standardized manner; or in issuing a permanent curriculum; or in creating modes of assessment that will travel. Several U.S. communities are trying the model in St. Louis, Missouri; Columbus, Ohio; Amherst, Massachusetts; Los Angeles; Des Moines Iowa; the District of Columbia, among others.

Comments: Effective in all developmental domains with an emphasis on creativity.

TABLE 5.3 Selected Innovative Teaching Strategies

BIBLIOTHERAPY
(Early Model from the 1980s)

(See, Cornett, C. and Cornett, C. 1980. *Bibliotherapy: The right book at the right time.* Bloomington, Ind.: Phi Delta Kappa Education Foundation, 1980.)

Target Grade(s) or Age(s): K-8

Program Treatment: Bibliotherapy can be defined as getting the right book to the right child at the right time for the right problem. It is reported to be uniquely suited to meet gifted students' needs because of their wide fund of information, advanced vocabularies, high reasoning abilities, empathy, interest in others, and love of and skill in reading.

Providing books to students that match their personality. Stories must hold the child's attention and arouse curiosity. Stories have moral messages.

Assessment & Reported Outcomes: The following affective changes are reported: empathy, positive attitudes, personal and social adjustment, positive self-image, relieving emotional pressures, developing new interests, promoting tolerance, respecting and accepting others, encouraging the realization that there is good in all people, and helping the reader to identify socially acceptable behavior. Through the stimulation of moral values, the student experiences a desire to emulate models.
One model that provides a good taxonomy of questions for discussion is that of Calvin Taylor. Taylor's levels include academic, creative, planning, predicting/forecasting, communicating, creating, and evaluating/decision making. These skill areas are utilized by teachers to establish 3 or more questions used to stimulate discussion.

Comments: Impacts the developmental domains of moral development, cognition, social and emotional development.

Enriching the Lives of Children

CELEBRITY INTERVIEWS

Target Grade(s) or Age(s): Elementary

Program Treatment: Each student is paired with another who is interviewed as if he or she were a celebrity. Typical questions asked are: What was your favorite activity in your early days of school? What is your secret to success?—among other questions.

This is a useful activity for a newly formed group or during the first days of class.

Assessment & Reported Outcomes: It is reported that gifted students have a great deal of fun telling about themselves and this activity brings out the student's sense of humor.

Comments: A great strategy for improving psychosocial development and self-esteem.

SCIENCE BEYOND THE CLASSROOM
(See Ramey-Gassert, 1997.)

Target Grade(s) or Age(s): K-6

Program Treatment: Science education reform documents a call for science to be taught in the manner that students learn best, by conducting hands-on, engaging investigations using simple everyday materials. Cited as being overlooked are informal science learning environments such as science centers, museums, and zoos, which provide students with captivating science experiences that can be related closely to curricular objectives.

The focus of this project is to provide informal science learning experiences in the context of a variety of out-of-school science environments, for children, and for in-service and pre-service teachers. Informal science education environments provide students with unique, engaging science learning opportunities and classroom teachers with a wealth of science teaching resources.

Examples of program strategies include the following:

-Kindergartners collected plant specimens, comparing similarities and differences between ones at the nature center/botanic garden and those in the school yard.

-A zoo naturalist helped student learn about native and exotic animals, and they compared these animals' bodies and lifestyles (families, communities) to their own.

-Third graders assisted the kindergartners with several of their schoolyard investigations.

-The first-grade teachers and students researched and developed a "museum" displaying science activities and content over a wide range of topics. The fourth graders shared their reading, listening, and writing expertise with the first-grade museum developers.

-Second-grade students and teachers obtained funding to set up a weather station on one corner of the school grounds, similar to one at the nature center. They collected and compiled weather data throughout the year and compared it to weather conditions 3 miles away at the center. With the help of the fifth graders, students presented this information to the whole school in a weekly and monthly chart displayed in the front hall. They also visited a local TV station to see the weather forecasting equipment and hosted periodic visits to their classroom by the TV weathercaster.

Assessment & Reported Outcomes: It is reported that museum learning nurtures curiosity; proves motivation and attitudes, engages the audience through participation and social interaction, and enrichment. By nurturing curiosity, the desire to learn can be enhanced.

Informal science learning environments allow students to observe and investigate natural objects and phenomena and live specimens in ways that textbooks cannot. Science centers combine space and time for reflection with exhibit areas that promote experiential involvement in learning.

Museums presuppose learners to be responsive, reflective, and observant visitors with prior knowledge and the ability to connect new information with their everyday lives. Museums assist people with the exploration and development of what they know and invite an avalanche of questions and foster the web work of connections that configurate a learning life. Museums draw heavily on the psychomotor domain with the presence of gadgets and technology that develop skills in manipulating manual dexterity, and hand-to-eye coordination. Also personally interacting with new material increases the acquisition and retention of information.

Enriching the Lives of Children

It is concluded that projects with appropriate scoring rubrics, where students combine science content from the classroom and museum are the best way for students to demonstrate learning. Museums are non evaluative, stimulating places to explore knowledge about the world that science and technology have generated.

Comments: The use of museums is an excellent and stimulating educational experience for students at all levels and in most subject areas. Most museums have specialists on hand to assist teaching faculty with designing meaningful teaching and learning experiences for students.

Early Arts Education (*Concept Model)
(See Bleiker, 1999).

Target Grade(s) or Age(s): Preschool & Elementary

Program Treatment: It is believed that children's art and drawings hold the key to understanding both cognitive and emotional development. Teachers are encouraged to incorporate art and drawing into the school curriculum on a regular basis. Students should be offered a visually and spatially rich environment in which they can interact.

Assessment & Reported Outcomes: Art is instrumental in developing the "self" in children.
Comments: More investigation of this area is needed to discover interesting and novel programs.

Higher Order Thinking Skills Project (H.O.T.S.)

Target Grade(s) or Age(s): Chapter 1 students in grades 4-6 in reading and math; Learning disabled students in grades 4-6 and gifted kids in grades K-2. Also grade 7 students.

Program Treatment: Replaces traditional drill and practice activities and content instruction in compensatory programs with thinking activities designed to generate the gains in basic skills. The goal is to provide students with conceptual skills to learn the more sophisticated content of the upper elementary grade levels the first time it is taught in the classroom.

Program is conducted in a lab, equipped with Apple Computers with a detailed curriculum and teacher trained in Socratic dialogue techniques. Computers are used to enhance motivation and improve students' ability to self-monitor their own comprehension. Curriculum provides dialogues to improve metacognition, inference from context, decontextualization, and information synthesis.

Assessment & Reported Outcomes: Students thinking abilities and social confidence are improved. Students' increased abilities to articulate ideas and engage in sophisticated conversations enhance their language use and ability to learn content, with gains in both reading and math.

Chapter 1 students in grades 4-6 improved their performance in reading and math to a greater extent than national averages and control groups, while also improving thinking ability as measured by the ROSS and Inference from Context measures. Improved self-concept and improved participation in content learning in the classroom were also evident.

Comments: Program designed to increase cognitive development.

Civic Virtues-Political Education (*Concept Model)
(See White, 1999).

Target Grade(s) or Age(s): K-12

Program Treatment: There is a need for citizenship education. Citizenship education needs to start from the values and associated institutional practices and civic virtues of liberal democracy. Citizens need political knowledge and skills but they also need to be certain sorts of people, to exercise civic virtues. The fostering of civic virtues can and should begin in the first school, primarily through its organization and ethos. Teachers need to be educated in preparation for this.

If the school is to be a democratic institution and educate its youngest students for democracy, its teachers need a nuanced understanding of democratic values and their associated institutional practices and the civic virtues which support them.

Enriching the Lives of Children

Assessment & Reported Outcomes: None reported.

Comments: An interesting concept.

CHESS CLUBS
Roberto Clemente Middle School, Bronx, NY

(See, Ferguson, *The Use and Impact of Chess* at: www.successchess.com/ChessResearch Summary. PDF; Ferguson, Robert. C. 2006. Teacher's guide: Research and benefits of chess. http://www.quadcitychess.com/benefits_of_chess.html; and McDonald, Patrick. 2006. The benefits of chess in education: A collection of studies and papers on chess and education. Canada: Ontario Chess Association. http://www.psmcd.ca/ftpfolder/BenefitsofChessIn EdScreen2.pdf.)

Target Grade(s) or Age(s): Middle School

Program Treatment: A competition that links school to the outside world. Chess is good for promoting critical thinking and logical reasoning. There are close links between cognition and perception. Children look for analogies and spot patterns which enables them to determine what is relevant. This also enables them to solve problems.

Assessment & Reported Outcomes: Improves concentration, enables students to think more carefully, anticipate the future. Allows for logical reasoning. Includes intuitive and analytical processes. Other documented impacts include: develops memory; teaches independence; promotes imagination and creativity; inspires self-motivation; improves schoolwork and grades; and, chess aids in developing thinking.

Comments: This particular program is world renown for its successful and stimulating strategies for motivating students and improving their academic ability. Many of these children live in lower socio-economic areas of New York City.

TABLE 5.4 Teaching for Multiple Intelligences – Models and Programs

VIRGINIA THINK TANK,
Kent Gardens Elementary School, McLean, VA
(See: Knodt, Jean. 1997.)

Target Grade(s) or Age(s): Elementary (K-6)

Program Treatment: All K-6 students flock to a hands-on discovery room – a place to explore all the ways of being smart. Faculty members and volunteer Room Guides (20-30 parents and community members) are trained to help out.

The Think Tank is a large room with a light and open atmosphere. Walk into a lab in progress and you see children engaged in a variety of group or individual activities. They may be working on a project at one of the round tables or at "Think It! Do It!" – the invention center. Some may be collaborating on "20 Questions," comfortably propped up on pillows. Others may be searching for objects to view under a microscope, making architectural drawings, or examining the way a door knob works. The spirit and tempo will vary from loud and active to pensive and quiet, but all the students seem to be having fun while working hard.

The Think Tank synthesizes many ideas and theories, including Socratic questioning, John Dewey (learning through doing), Project Spectrum-linking assessment to meaningful, real-world activities and emphasizing children's strengths. There also is a flow activities room (Csikszentmihalyi).

The Think Tank has "flow" as it offers children a choice of diverse, challenging activities and opportunities to develop and practice process-oriented skills and the capacity for sustained absorption in an activity. All activities in the Think Tank are integrated with all other coursework. Room Guides help students discover connections and link learning in the lab to their school curriculum and to their home and community experiences. Some students continue projects in their classrooms or at home and teach others what they have learned in the lab. Younger children often build projects that older children have left in the lab. When possible, students of various ages work together. To extend the learning experience essential questions are posed that stimulate creative problem solving and critical, higher-order thinking while connecting learning to the county's required program of studies.

Assessment & Reported Outcomes: No mention of assessment or of student outcomes. To be investigated.

Comments: An interesting model using many of the recommended constructivists strategies for learning.

Enriching the Lives of Children

THE KEY LEARNING COMMUNITY
Indianapolis, Indiana
(See description under Table 5.2-Programs)

THE BRAIN-FLEX PROJECT,
New South Wales, Australia

Target Grade(s) or Age(s): Middle School

Program Treatment: In Australia, students at a coeducational Catholic school are pursuing individualized projects that promote lifelong learning skills. This multiple intelligences-based program has generated many projects. An academically gifted 14 year-old learned the skills of horse dressage; a Year 8 student with learning difficulties demonstrated to the principal the model plane he had designed and built; and a group of girls and boys cooked family recipes (and then tested them on the Head of Curriculum.)

These students pursue independent projects for nearly two hours every two weeks. The program is designed to encourage independent learning among early secondary school students. Each student completes 2-3 projects per year.

Assessment & Reported Outcomes: No description of assessment provided, but an interesting concept. A set of conclusions are offered: people learn best when the subject really interest them; people learn in different ways; how people learn must always be appropriate to what is being learned; and, students develop as learners when they are responsible for their own learning.

Comments: The emphasis on education for self and life-long development is important.

NEW CANAAN PUBLIC SCHOOL, SUMMER CAMP
"The Summer Stars Program"- Connecticut.
(See Cantrell, et al., 1997.

Target Grade(s) or Age(s): Elementary school, ages 7-12 years.

Program Treatment: A one-week summer camp where children can tap into their unique strengths. Students participate in choosing materials and activities from many different topics and participating in one of three internships: the Challenger Mission at Bridgeport Discovery Museum, the Sea Voyage at Norwalk Maritime Center, or simulated flight training at the Sikorsky Aircraft Corporation in Stratford.

The camp respects children's multiple intelligences and problem-solving competencies and their potential to maximize their multiple "smarts." Projects include: producing a handcrafted bound book, writing musical compositions, constructing rockets, building block structures from students' blueprints, writing and illustrating a camp newsletter, and reinventing stories to tell at the closing ceremony. Children also work on motion experiments, prepare astronaut food, produce and act in plays and design T-shirts.

Assessment & Reported Outcomes: Survey data suggest conclusively that the camp's application of multiple intelligence theory positively affects children's understanding of their perceived "smarts," promotes risk-taking, and closes the gap between parents' and students' understanding of the theory.

Comments: A meaningful summer enrichment program for children.

AUSTRALIA PUBLIC SCHOOLS
(See Vaille, 1997.)

Target Grade(s) or Age(s): Preschool, Kindergarten and Primary School.

Program Treatment: Multiple intelligences theory has transformed teaching in Australia, according to a survey of 30 schools Gifted education has been enriched as well. The theory also is widely used in training programs in business and industry.

Enriching the Lives of Children

The system develops integrated units from mind maps to MI Olympics. Each Olympics session is a celebration of students' diverse abilities, where all intelligences and all classes are represented. These offer a broad range of classroom activities while promoting the connections across disciplines that make learning more meaningful. Teachers select an appropriate theme, such as Fantasy or Refugees or the Human Body. They then plan activities that will require students to use all of the intelligences, as well as cover all the key learning areas.

Assessment & Reported Outcomes: Teachers and student are mutually engaged in planning, implementing, observing, and reflecting on their mutual work. Students can also opt to work on independent projects. In one assessment, the students who completed independent projects received higher marks than they had on previous tests.

Comments: The Australian public school system is advancing in reporting innovative models for learning.

REGGIO EMILIA, ITALY-APPROACH TO PRESCHOOL EDUCATION
Twenty-two municipal preschools and thirteen infant and toddler day care centers (Gardner 1999).
(See program description in Table 5.2.)

TABLE 5.5 Inquiry and Problem-Based Models

INQUIRING SCIENTISTS
(See Colburn, 2004).

Target Grade(s) or Age(s): K-12

Program Treatment: Deeply rooted in best practices, inquiry-based teaching is designed to help students learn to think independently and gain problem-solving skills that will help them throughout life. By prompting students to come up with their own answers, inquiry-based instruction leads to a deeper understanding of scientific concepts. To gain a deep understanding of scientific concepts, learners must actively grapple with the content.

Inquiry-based learning is based on the principle of discovery. There are 3 types: Structured inquiry, guided inquiry and open inquiry. In open inquiry, students make almost all the decisions, such as when a student completes a science fair project.

Assessment & Reported Outcomes: The goals of scientific reasoning and critical thinking are assessed. Also continual formative assessment of student understanding through observation, student questioning, and written assignments are used as assessment tools. Teachers can also assess students' abilities to: generate open-ended, researchable queries; devise scientific procedures; and, interpret data.

Comments: The end result of learning and assessment is the type of product or exhibit students fashion based on their understanding.

ENRICHMENT CLUSTERS
(Bret Harte Middle School, Oakland, CA)
(See Renzuli, Gentry, & Reis, 2004)

Target Grade(s) or Age(s): Elementary/Middle

Program Treatment: Students leave their classroom to participate in interest-based enrichment clusters. Under a teacher's guidance, one group of students is identifying, archiving, and preserving documents from the 1800s that were found in a suitcase belonging to the first pharmacist in Deadwood, South Dakota. Another group with strong interests in media, technology, and graphic

Enriching the Lives of Children

arts is converting the archives into digital format and making the students' research available on a Web site.

These cross-grade clusters are scheduled on a rotating basis during each semester and last for 8 weeks, meeting weekly for a double-period time block. A medium-sized school might typically offer 15 to 20 clusters. The number of students varies depending upon their interest in the topic and teacher requirements for effective student participation.

Teachers develop clusters around their own strengths and interests, sometimes working in teams that include parents and community members. It is reported that many schools across the U.S. have developed the enrichment clusters to make learning more meaningful and authentic. In these clusters, the nature of the problem guides students toward using just-in-time knowledge, appropriate investigative techniques or creative production of skills, and professional methods for communicating results.

Students assume roles of investigators, writers, artists, and other types of practicing professionals. The student's role changes from lesson-learner to firsthand inquirer and the role of the teacher changes from instructor and disseminator of knowledge to coach, resource procurer and mentor. Students learn from the cognitive, affective and motivational processes involved.

Assessment & Reported Outcomes: No discussion of formal assessment was provided.

Comments: Affects all cognitive domains.

THE RIVER CITY PROJECT
(**Multi-User Virtual Environment Experiential Simulator**), **Harvard University**
(See, http://muve.gse.harvard.edu/rivercityproject)
(See also, Dede, et al. 2005.)

Target Grade(s) or Age(s): K-12

Program Treatment: River City, is an interactive computer simulation of a town in the 1800s, uses Multi-User Virtual Environment (MUVE) technology to enhance student learning and motivation in science.

A MUVE is a virtual environment where multiple participants can explore, communicate, accomplish tasks, and progress through various levels of the world simultaneously.

River City uses an interactive medium to motivate and support all school students to learn science content and inquiry skills, regardless of their previous successes or failures. No special technology knowledge is necessary for teacher or students. The program focuses on the areas of epidemiology, scientific inquiry and experimentation. It is interdisciplinary in scope, spanning the domains of ecology, health, biology, chemistry, earth science and history.

Students encounter clues to a problem plaguing the 19th century River City-three diseases affect health of the residents. Students can form and test hypotheses, design experiments, make quantitative and qualitative observations, gather data, make graphs and tables, draw inferences, make conclusions, develop written research reports, share report findings and critique their process and results.

Assessment & Reported Outcomes: Findings show that learned biology content, students and teachers were highly engaged, that student attendance improved and disruptive behavior dropped. Further students were able to build 21st century skills in virtual communication and expression.

Comments: A virtual learning experience for students.

TABLE 5.6 Science Models

SCIENCE BEYOND THE CLASSROOM
(K-6)
(See Ramey-Gassert, 1997.)
See Program Description in Table 5.3.

GLOBE
(K-12)
(Global Learning and Observations to Benefit the Environment Program)
An international program. Website: www.globe.gov.

Enriching the Lives of Children

See Program Description in Table 5.2.

THE RIVER CITY PROJECT
(K-12)
(Multi-User Virtual Environment Experiential Simulator, Harvard University)
(See, http://muve.gse.harvard.edu/rivercityproject)
(See also, Dede, et al. 2005.)
See Program Description in Table 5.5.

INQUIRING SCIENTISTS
(K-12)
(See Colburn 2004.)
See Program Description in Table 5.5.

TABLE 5.7 Service and Field-Based Models

CAMPUS CALGARY/OPEN MINDS PROGRAM
(Canada)
(See Cochrane, 2004.)

Target Grade(s) or Age(s): K-12

Program Treatment: Program gives public school and private school teachers at all levels the chance to move their classrooms to one of nine community sites for a week of powerful project-based learning. Students learn and connect to knowledgeable adults in a real-world setting. Through hands-on experience and personal connection with adults in the community along with the freedom to write and reflect on their experience, students learn at a deeper level than is possible solely in the classroom.

The model consists of a partnership between local school boards, community sites, and corporate sponsors who provide financial support—including Chevron Texaco, Petro-Canada, the City of Calgary, the Stampede Foundation, University of Calgary, and the Canadian Olympic Development Association. Most participants are public elementary school students.

Creative artists coach teachers in brining out children's creativity—leading teachers themselves in intensive journal writing—because the Campus Calgary model values student writing and drawing as a path to authentic learning. A major principle of the program is that writing and drawing can lead students into the process of discovering, thinking, and learning. Combining visual and written expression allows students to explore creatively and extends their ability to say what they really mean, as reflected in their journal entries.

Assessment & Reported Outcomes: Assessment has largely focused on one particular ability—the ability to communicate ideas through writing. Researchers tested the writing skills of 266 students from twelve 3rd grade classrooms. Half of these 4th graders then took part in Campus Calgary, and the other half in regular school programs. The Campus Calgary group and the control group had similar initial writing scores. After exposure to the program, students who took part in the program improved by an average of 24 percent as compared to 6 percent for the control group.

It is reported that the model has now spread across North America and beyond. The program has been replicated at Aqua School in Vancouver, British Columbia, and Open Minds in Singapore.

Comments: Much work is done around the concept of "story." Students learn how to look deeply at artifacts and use them as launching points for stories that inform people about the world. Rather than responding to teacher-assigned topics, they become keen to share stories related to their personal experiences at the site.

Examples of activities include: at the science centre school, students exploring freezing and melting temperatures; at the University school, students observing, sketching and interpreting sculptures; at the City Hall school, students compare a model of downtown Calgary with observations made earlier on a walking tour of the city; and, at Aerospace School, students assemble the motor for a remote control airplane.

Enriching the Lives of Children

TABLE 5.8 Innovative Instructional Technology Models

PROGRAMMABLE BRICKS
(Massachusetts Institute of Technology, Media Laboratory)
(See Resnick, 2000.)

Target Grade(s) or Age(s): K-6+

Program Treatment: Programmable bricks are tiny computers embedded inside children's building blocks. With these bricks, children can build computational power directly into their physical world constructions, blurring the boundaries between the physical and digital worlds.

In pilot studies, children have used programmable bricks to build a variety of creative constructions, including an odometer for roller blades (using a magnetic sensor to count wheel rotations), a diary security system (using a touch sensor to detect if anyone tried to open the diary), and an automated hamster cage (using a light sensor to monitor the hamster's movements during the day). One student built a new type of bird feeder that could take a picture of the bird when it landed on the feeder.

Assessment & Reported Outcomes: Project serves as a rich context for engaging in scientific inquiry and learning science-related concepts. Students develop a deeper understanding of concepts and get hands on experience.

Comments: Designer of program indicates that new computer technologies will require new educational strategies and new public polices, along with new public understanding of the nature of learning. Affects all developmental domains; but especially cognition and creativity.

MICROCOMPUTER-BASED LABORATORY IN CREEK BIOLOGY
Website: http://probesight.concord.org, or http://www.concord.org~sherry/cilt

Target Grade(s) or Age(s): K-6

Program Treatment: Two sixth-grade classes use palmtop computers with chemical sensors attached and head out for a field trip to the local creek. Today with palmtop computers, students can measure the creek and see the results of their data gathering while still in the field. The computers store and graph the data immediately, allowing students to see how the graphs unfold in real time, directly related to their observations.

The immediacy of this process helps students understand what the graph's time axis means, a challenge for many students who have only recently learned how to plot points.

Assessment & Reported Outcomes: Students are able to develop their critical thinking skills by analyzing their initial results and running follow-up experiments.

Comments: A stimulating and active learning process.

COMPUTER-SUPPORTED INTENTIONAL LEARNING ENVIRONMENT (CSILE) PROJECT
Website: http://csile.oise.utoronto.ca.

Target Grade(s) or Age(s): K-12

Program Treatment: CSILE is a community database that students use to share their findings as they do research alone, in small groups, as a whole class, or across classrooms. Students work with teachers to develop researchable questions based on both library research and real-world observations or experiments. As students pursue questions they find interesting, they put their ideas, questions, and findings into the CSILE software systems as notes and share them with their peers across the ocean. Notes are classified into types of thinking such as "My theory for now…" or "What I need to know next is…"

Through interaction with teachers and peers, students are able to refine their ideas online. Students can express their ideas in both text and graphics; and students use a mix of languages, such as English, Inuit, and Finnish.

Assessment & Reported Outcomes: It is reported that students gain better writing and language skills and increased multicultural understanding. Students in K-12 classes who use CSILE for science, history, and social studies perform better on standardized tests and create deeper explanations than students in classes without this technology. Positive effects are especially strong for low and middle achieving students.

Enriching the Lives of Children

Reports from researchers and teachers suggest that students who participate in computer-connected learning networks show increased motivation, a deeper understanding of concepts, and an increased willingness to tackle difficult questions.

Comments: In addition to reaching the developmental domains, such a program also teaches students the importance of civic responsibility and contributing to the good of humankind by sharing and exchanging information on what one has learned.

GLOBE
(K-12)
(Global Learning and Observations to Benefit the Environment Program)
An international program. Website: www.globe.gov.
See Program Description in Table 5.2.

THINKER-TOOLS

Website: http://thinkertools.berkeley.edu:7019.

Target Grade(s) or Age(s): Middle School

Program Treatment: Students use ThinkerTools to view simulated objects on a screen, where they can adjust the settings to better understand the laws of physics. ThinkerTools shows students what they cannot see in the real world.

Simulated objects on the screen move according to the laws of physics (with or without gravity and friction, depending on the settings). The big difference is that the computer can superimpose arrows representing force, acceleration, and/or velocity, so that for the first time students can actually "see" the equation $F=ma$. Students can also change these arrows themselves to get a more intuitive sense of forces and motion.

Assessment & Reported Outcomes: In controlled studies, researchers found that middle school students who used Thinker Tools developed the ability to give correct scientific explanations of Newtonian principles several grade levels before the concept usually is taught.

Middle school students who participated in ThinkerTools outperformed high school physics students in their ability to apply the basic principles of Newtonian mechanics to real-world situations: the middle school students averaged 68% correct answers on a six-item, multiple-choice test, compared with 50% for the high school physics students.

Comments: A great and creative way to teach students the concepts of physics so they can be grasped and understood. This project reminds this author of the *Physics is Fun* project sponsored by the Physics Department at the University of Maryland at College Park, MD.

SIMCALC

Website: www.simcalc.umassd.edu

Target Grade(s) or Age(s): Middle School

Program Treatment: A software application for students learning the basics of calculus. Using a SimCalc animation of a clown walking along a road and software that related graphs of the motion to the animation itself, students can explore the difference between constant velocity and constant acceleration.

Students can easily relate mathematical symbols either to data from the real world or to simulations of familiar phenomena, giving the mathematics a greater sense of meaning. Students can receive feedback when they create a notation that is incorrect; and the computer can beep if a student tries to sketch a nonsensical math function in a graph.

Assessment & Reported Outcomes: The Project has shown that computers can help middle school students learn calculus concepts such as rate, accumulation, limit, and mean value.

Research findings show that inner-city middle school students—many of whom ordinarily would be weeded out of mathematics before reaching this level—were able to surpass the efforts of college students in their understanding of fundamental concepts of calculus, based on a SimCalc assessment examining conceptual understanding of calculus.

Comments: Calculus is difficult for students to grasp, especially the concepts behind the formulas and equations. This software provides students with conceptual models and understanding of concepts.

Enriching the Lives of Children

DIGITAL STORYTELLING
(See Ohler, 2005 & 2006.)

Target Grade(s) or Age(s): K-6

Program Treatment: Through creating electronic personal narratives, students become active creators, rather than passive consumers, of multimedia. Students can also video record themselves and place themselves in the story. Through creating narratives, students develop the power of their own voices.

Digital stories can be used to strengthen students' critical thinking, report writing, and media literacy skills. They also become heroes of their own learning stories.

Assessment & Reported Outcomes: Digital storytelling helps students become active participants rather than passive consumers in a society saturated with media. Digital stories provide powerful media literacy learning opportunities because students are involved in the creation and analysis of the media in which they are immersed.

Comments: All forms of storytelling are powerful forms of learning on all developmental levels for students.

GEN YES MENTORING MODEL
Website: www.genyes.com.
(See Chuang and Thompson, 2006.)

Target Grade(s) or Age(s): Grades 3-12

Program Treatment: This program has developed and implemented an instructional technology support model that includes authentic involvement of students in grades 3-12. Instead of having teachers take online courses or attend workshops or college courses for professional development in technology integration, the program makes it possible for students to mentor teachers and serve as resources at the teachers' schools.

The GenYES model trains students to provide continual on-site content-related technology support to teachers. Secondary school students take training courses for 18 weeks and elementary school children take course for 30 weeks.

Elementary students at one school in Maryland, who completed the training, were paired with a partner teacher. Together teacher and student decided which unit or lesson might be enhanced by including technology. Students suggested a variety of approaches to incorporating technology into the lesson; including finding appropriate Web sites and helping teachers learn to use fitting applications—for example, PowerPoint for presentations, Kidspiration to form a concept map, and Kid Pix to create a slide show.

Another group of GenYES elementary students helped their partner teachers create a video-embedded PowerPoint project in a visual arts lesson on sculpture. Student mentors first conducted research on the Internet and then visited the National Gallery of Art in Washington, DC to take photographs of sculptures. The PowerPoint presentation included photographs, text about the sculptors, and a step-by-step video to help students create sculptures of their own. Exposed to both text and video formats, students learned to develop and apply criteria to evaluate their own and others' artwork. Partner teachers learned how to insert a movie into a PowerPoint slide and were able to teach students to insert a video into their electronic portfolios during a subsequent lesson.

Assessment & Reported Outcomes: Students benefit by developing their technical, collaborative, and leadership skills. One teacher reported that her student mentor went from barely participating in class to explaining, demonstrating, and teaching computer procedures and programs. Using students to mentor teachers also is a powerful way to celebrate and capitalize on intergenerational differences.

Comments: A powerful way to learn—through teaching others. When we teach, we also learn.

ROBOTIC PETS
(See Melson, 2006.)

Target Grade(s) or Age(s): Ages 7-14

Program Treatment: One project has developed robotic pets to study the interaction patterns and development of social competence and moral development. In the study children interact in separate sessions with a live pet and with a robotic dog. Sessions are video-taped. Researchers are asking questions in 4 major areas: Children's concepts of physical essences, e.g. does AIBO have a brain? Children's concepts of agency and mental states, e.g., can AIBO feel scared? Children's concepts of social companionship, e.g., Can AIBO be your friend? and, Children's moral concepts, e.g., should AIBO be blamed?' Can he be punished?' Is it all right to hit AIBO?

Enriching the Lives of Children

Assessment & Reported Outcomes: No assessment information provided.

Comments: Additional research is needed on this project.

THE RIVER CITY PROJECT
(K-12)
(Multi-User Virtual Environment Experiential Simulator, Harvard University)
(See http://muve.gse.harvard.edu/rivercityproject)
(See also, Dede, et al. 2005.)
See Program Description in Table 5.5.

Table 5.9 Projects with a Global Focus

GLOBAL EDUCATION (JORDAN)
(See El- Sheikh Hasan, 2000.)

Target Grade(s) or Age(s): K-12

Program Treatment: Jordan has developed and implemented a comprehensive educational reform project aimed at improving the quality of school learning and teaching. The project calls for a school curriculum that is differentiated to meet students' diversity, promote critical thinking skills, relates school learning to work and life, and enables students to use school learning in problem solving and decision-making.

The Global Education Program (GEP), which started as an experimental project in four schools during the academic year 1992-93, is being implemented in more than 40 schools all over Jordan.

The aim of the program is to empower learners and involve them in transformative social action, at the local, regional, and world levels, and to build a world based on human dignity, justice, equity, and freedom. It is an innovative pedagogy that focuses on empowering students to learn and grow through developing their social and emotional learning skills, cultivating their cognitive skills and strategies, and promoting their awareness of interrelatedness among peoples, environments, and cultures.

Students are presented real life-like situations which are followed by a set of probing questions that encourage them to intellectually and emotionally interact with the situation. Scenarios may include verbal (oral and written), pictorial, or action modes. They may complete open-ended stories, the combining of parts to form whole, perspective taking, moral reasoning, role playing, proposing solutions, futuristic thinking and more.

Assessment & Reported Outcomes: No assessment offered.

Comments: No examples or scenarios of the program are provided. Further research need to be conducted on this project, but the concept is an interesting one.

TRAVEL SCHOOLING
*Concept Model
(See Byrnes, 2001.)

Target Grade(s) or Age(s): K-12

Program Treatment: Travel schooling is defined as the education provided children who are traveling for days, weeks, or even months during the normal academic year, with parents or guardians. Travel schooling takes planning, creativity, hard work, and flexibility.

The author provides a set of strategies for making the travel educationally beneficial, including: an exploration of literature and books; selecting historical fiction, movies and films; having students do reflective writing and collecting items for a scrapbook; journaling; Visual records of the trip with photographs, sketchbooks, video camera; an alphabet log to describe something about the culture, beginning with "A;" collecting culture specific artifacts; learning map reading and geography; and more.

Assessment & Reported Outcomes: Children learn much and become globally knowledgeable, with cross-cultural perspectives. Children can also produce products, such as travel stories, photographic journals and more.

Enriching the Lives of Children

Comments: This concept was presented by a parent who had the challenge of educating her child while pulling him out of school for travel. Similarly, study abroad tours and programs could benefit from many of the suggestions offered.

WORLD LITERATURE
(See Stan, 1999.)

Target Grade(s) or Age(s): K-12

Program Treatment: The model emphasizes the importance of importing children's literature from other countries besides the more industrialized countries that share our world view. The research recommends that the most appropriate age to introduce global perspectives is at the elementary level.

Assessment & Reported Outcomes: The benefit of having children read global literature is to increase international understanding. Encountering a country through the perspective of a character that lives there creates a personal relationship with a place not possible through a textbook or television encounter.

Comments: This would be particularly impactful at the elementary level. Students at upper levels are more likely to get exposure to literature from across the world.

NEW WORLDQUEST
A Game to Promote Global Understanding
(See, http://www.psyking.net/id225.htm.)

Target Grade(s) or Age(s): All ages.

Program Treatment: Games are a unique way to model strategies and interactions among individuals. Games can also solve major crises, train war heroes, and more.

"New WorldQuest" is a problem-solving simulation and action game. The game is designed to promote communication and global understanding between diverse student populations in the classroom and other educational settings; The game has been piloted in different contexts at the college level. The game will also be piloted at the elementary through high school levels.

The game is designed to encourage the shaping of cognition and behavior and to stimulate the thinking of students toward creating a new paradigm on building global understanding. The new paradigm helps students to understand the importance of communication, cooperation, building cooperative structures; and, moving across differences, to resolve conflicts and cooperatively developing strategies and programs for the betterment of the nation and world. An overview of the game can be described as follows:

A new world order is being created in an effort to transform humankind, bring peace to the world, and build coalitions and a new economic structure. An advisory body of representative leaders from each nation across the world is meeting to develop visionary plans regarding the essential components of this "new world order." The group consists of scientists, social scientists, planners, technologists, economists, and other professionals. They have formed a new corporation called The New WorldQuest Federation. The Federation has been given the authority by the United Nations to develop all rules and guidelines governing the new codes of conduct and international relations. The Federation has called for the forming of national and international coalitions representing diverse groups to plan and develop proposals for the creation of this new world order.

They are particularly interested in coalitions addressing how they will transform the current world community, create working coalitions, and promote peace and productivity worldwide. Students playing the game volunteer to work in one or several coalitions charged with creating the new world order. Coalitions include: Education; Social System; Health, Food & Nutrition; Technology & Communication Systems; Economic Structure; Political & Governing Structure; Transportation; Energy & Power Plants; and the Military.

Assessment & Reported Outcomes: See student comments of the effects of the game on their learning online. Game promotes cognitive, language, moral, social and emotional development, as well as creativity and leadership skills.

Comments: This game is designed for individuals of all ages, but has been pilot tested on community college students to date.

CONCLUSIONS

This book has explored the research literature on innovative and novel ways to enrich the lives of children's learning within and outside of the classroom. The goal has been to seek explanations about the ways to maximize learning, growth and development for children in all the developmental domains—cognitive, moral, social, and emotional. The development of creativity is examined as well as the importance of achieving some level of independence in learning.

After reviewing a substantial body of literature reflecting constructivists, cognitive developmental and authentic learning models, it is interesting to note that the literature reveals a shift or transition occurring over the past 2 decades in perspectives, models and approaches. Further, there seems to be a collective movement, worldwide, to at least investigate or explore strategies and programs that could improve the academy of teaching and learning. While the perspectives and models found are of moderate proportion, there are an increasing number of educators who are actively seeking new ways to engage students in learning. This researcher was very pleased with the excitement conveyed by educators in the field as they described their models.

Key Findings

Traditional vs. Innovative Ideology

- There is an ideological divide in education with those who emphasize traditional modes of teaching and learning vs. those that emphasize the need for learning to be constructed, authentic, meaningful, and understood.

- Others believe we can have the best of both worlds and they have coined the term "innovative traditionalism."

Meaning of Enrichment

- No significant definition of "enrichment" was found; and therefore, this researcher defined enrichment as: *"Improving the quality and value of one's life through nurturance and development of one's human potential by provision of stimulating experiences that energize the individual to act in positive and productive ways; and, with the end result being enhanced growth and development that leads to a higher quality of life, greater productivity, balance and wholeness."*

- The call to enrich the lives of children is the call to give the children of the world every opportunity to evolve into psychologically healthy, whole, viable, and productive human beings, who will contribute to the good of self, society and world.

Theoretical Propositions: Authentic Pedagogy, Constructing Knowledge, Teaching for Meaning and Understanding

- Theoretical propositions in support of enriching children's lives call for teaching and learning that is authentic and allows children to personally construct knowledge and meaning with use of conceptual tools. This is not a new concept as early philosophers, psychologists, and educators have advocated some of these same notions.

- Early scholars such as Aristotle, Husserl, Vygotsky, Piaget and Bruner pointed to the necessity of students being able to socially construct meaning and understanding through learning.

- Currently, there is a growing group of scholars supporting the constructivist philosophy about learning, with variations (Gardner, Newmann, Csikszentmihalyi, Sternberg, Feldman, and others. These scholars support the notion that finding ways to stimulate children's educational lives is important.

- Likewise, many scholars emphasize the importance and connections between learning, meaning and understanding. Research reviewed over the last 30 years reveals that learning for meaning leads to greater retention and use of information and ideas. The goal of education should have at its core, meaning making.

Interrelationship between Learning and Developmental Domains: Cognitive, Moral, Social/Emotional, Physical and Brain Development

- It is the prevailing notion that learning is a part of the developmental domains. There is an interconnection between learning, cognition, social and emotional development. Therefore, when we speak about stimulating children's lives, strategies that are developed must also address the developmental domains.

- Further, it is believed that learning and development must occur for other reasons than just academic performance. Learning should also have effects outside of school, in life.

- There has been a great deal of focus on learning, development and brain research. For example, we know that there are physiological linkages to learning and corresponding brain changes as one engages in the activity of learning. Further, the developmental domains impact brain growth, development and functioning as well.

- Research also reveals that the brain responds to environmental stimuli, much like people. Therefore, research now connects appropriate developmental practices with recent brain research findings. Learning does not take place as separate and isolated events. Brain, body and developmental domains work together. This book documents in detail, the findings on learning, development and brain connections, along with suggestions for appropriate classroom teaching and learning strategies.

- The development of moral character has been advocated in the earliest of times by scholars such as Dewey, Durkheim, Piaget, C.S. Lewis, Theodore Roosevelt and others. Further, it is known that cognitive development precedes moral reasoning and the development of character. Therefore, helping individuals understand moral behavior, as part of the learning process is imperative for a variety of reasons.

- The new character education partnership, as part of a national movement in the U.S., is attempting to reinstitute the importance of promoting cognitive, moral and character development; and, program developers are reporting very positive results as new instructional programs in the schools are implemented. Included in this book are some interesting suggestions about novel and stimulating activities that would encourage development of moral reasoning and character.

- Surprisingly, there is much in the research literature on the importance of stimulating healthy and positive emotional development in children. Moreover, emotions permeate everything that we do; and, affect our reactions to self and others. Stimulating educational experiences can trigger the sensory and emotional states of individuals in positive ways. This book points to some of the research findings related to impacts on emotional development.

- The research literature also makes distinctions about the cultural contexts of social, emotional and cognitive development and what specific cultures value or deem important.

- An important emphasis in the literature on emotional and social development is the importance of teaching children how to manage their emotions and to have positive, stable and balanced emotional grounding. Further, the research indicates that the teaching and learning of emotional development should be an integral part of the curriculum. Strategies such as cooperative learning are emphasized to promote positive emotional development.

- Social and emotional learning programs, then, seem to provide students with basic skills for success, not just in school but also in their personal, professional and civic lives.

Importance and Nature of Creativity and Relationship to Development

- One would be remiss in examining novel and stimulating environments and programs for children without talking about the importance of creativity. While many know little about the nature of creativity, a small group of scholars are actively conducting ongoing inquiries into its nature.

- It was determined decades ago, by Lev Vygotsky, that creativity is part of the developmental domain and interrelated to cognitive and emotional development. Moreover, creativity or the need to create seems to be an essential part of development. Further, there is a precise relationship between play and the development of creativity.

- Therefore, developing opportunities for the cultivation of creativity and structuring and creating opportunities for play seem to be essential and probably brain-based.

- This book delineates in detail the early notions of Lev Vygotsky on the elements and nature of creativity, creative imagination, play, and their relationship to development. Further, the research describes at length the importance of pretend and structured play and their contributions to the development of creative talent.

- The research also provides suggestions and strategies for teachers and parents to encourage and help children develop creativity. The research literature also points to the fact that when teachers use triarchical teaching strategies which include analytical, creative and practical learning, that not only does it improve students' creative domains, but also improves overall performance.

Structures and Strategies for Creating Enriching and Novel Stimulus Experiences

- An examination has been made of the particular strategies that might be used for creating novel stimulus experiences for children.

- In addition to the emphasis on constructing knowledge, using authentic pedagogy and teaching for meaning and understanding, the prevailing recommendations were to use a holistic approach, teach for development of the multiple intelligences, consider the incorporation of guided discovery, make opportunity for structured and pretend play, develop an environment for "flow" in what students are engaged in, differentiate instruction, and figure out how to use innovative technology as an instructional tool vs. the mechanics of technology.

- Many suggested strategies are provided in this book that would contribute to providing stimulating experiences for children, including the above-mentioned areas and strategies.

Selected Innovative and Workable Models

- Finally, a search for workable models and programs was undertaken to identify instruction designed to stimulate and provide novel educational experiences for children. Select samples of innovative programs from around the world are presented.

- Program models were found that fall into the following categories: large-scale, national and international programs; strategies for use in the classroom; the teaching and use of multiple intelligences in the classroom; inquiry- and problem-based learning; interesting and innovative science programs; service and field-based programs; innovative technology programs; and, programs that emphasize global understanding. Overviews of these programs are presented in this book.

Gaps in the Research

This state of the art assessment probably will be an ongoing process as new programs are identified and assessed. It is important to point out that due to the volume of information and findings, select areas of interest were omitted from this exploration, including a closer look at the research literature on the arts and the gifted and talented. These areas were tabled for future study.

An exploration is needed of those educators who may be developing interesting and novel educational games to engage the young child's mind as opposed to many of the current videogames.

This research provides a good assessment of the discussion and recommendations over the last two decades, since the call for reforms in education; but it does not include a comprehensive inclusion of pilot or newer models that may be on the horizon since this investigation. Recent innovative models should be explored.

It is this researcher's intention, that this body of findings will be the beginning of continued study that also will include an examination of enriching experiences for students at the secondary and postsecondary levels, using the same research framework. The ultimate goal is to gain a comprehensive understanding of the research theories, prescriptions and best practices in usable volumes for teaching, parenting and professional development at the elementary, postsecondary and higher educational levels.

The findings revealed to date, has truly been an enjoyable experience for this researcher and author. Never before has an attempt been made to synthesize the theoretical notions and models being piloted or implemented, worldwide. This exploration presents an exciting opportunity to contribute to discussions about the excitement and future sustainability of education in the twenty-first century and beyond.

Enriching the lives of children, in essence, will enrich the lives of society and world; and, lead to a productive and sustainable future for generations to come.

NOTES

[1] See, e.g., Case, R. & Okamoto, Y. (1996). The role of central conceptual structures in the development of children's thought. *Monographs of the Society for Research on Child Development*, 61(1-2, Serial No.246). In a review of cross-cultural research, these researchers found that children living in societies where the base ten number system is not in use, or where formal schooling is not available to all, they do not usually attain the level of formal operational thought normally reached by adults in industrial societies. To the extent that concrete operational reasoning is less valued, or less often necessary for daily existence, it may also be less apparent in children's daily activities and may develop later than in cultures where it is highly valued.

In another study by Dasen et al. (1985) where they conducted ethnographic research, they found two "emic" or native categories of intelligence among the Baoulé people living on the Ivory Coast. The first they classified as technological or scholarly and included skills such as observation, attention, memory, literacy, and schooling success. The second was referred to as "social" and included skills or characteristics such as politeness, helpfulness to others, verbal self-expression, responsibility, memory, and wisdom. Interestingly, the researchers state that this second type of intelligence was what was most valued by the Baoulé because they considered these qualities more relevant and useful to the functioning of the community.

See, Dasen, P.R., Barthélémy, D., Kan, E. Kouamé, K., Daouda, K., Adjéi, K. K., & Assandé, N. (1985). N'Glouele, l'intelligence chez les Baoulé [N'Glouele, intelligence according to the Baoulé]. *Archives de psychologie*, 53: 292-324.

REFERENCES

Alesandrini, Kathryn and Linda Larson. 2002. Teachers bridge to constructivism. *The Clearing House,* January/February: 118-121.

American Academy of Pediatrics. 2000. *Understanding the impact of media on children and teens.* http://www.aap.org/family/mediaimpact.htm.

Ancess, Jacqueline. 2004. Snapshots of meaning-making classrooms. Educational Leadership 62, no. 1(September 2004): 36-40.

Anderson, John R., James G. Greeno, Lynne M. Reder and Herbert A. Simon. 2000. Perspectives on learning, thinking and activity. *Educational Researcher,* 29:11-13.

Apple Classrooms of Tomorrow. 1995. *Changing the conversation about teaching, learning & technology: A report on 10 years of ACOT research.* Cupertino, CA: Apple Computer.

Armstrong, Thomas. 2006. *The best schools: How human development research should inform educational practice.* Alexandria, VA:ASCD.

—. 2007. The curriculum superhighway. *Educational Leadership,* 64:16-20.

Barron, F. & Harrington, D.M. 1981. Creativity, intelligence, and personality. *Annual Review of Psychology,* 32, 439-476.

Beatty, B. 2000. Children in different and difficult times: The history of American childhood, Part one. *History of Education Quarterly,* 40: 71-84.

Bereth, D. and M.Scherer.1993. On transmitting values: A conversation with Amitai Etzioni. *Educational Leadership* 51:12-15.

Bergen, Doris & Coscia, Juliet. 2001. Brain research and childhood education: Implications for educators. Olney, MD: Association for Childhood Education International.

Bergen, D. 2002. The role of pretend play in children's cognitive development. *Early Childhood Research and Practice,* 4: 1-13. http://ecrp.uiuc.edu/v4n1/bergen.html.

Berger, P.L. & Luckmann, T. 1967. The social construction of reality. Harmondsworth: Penguin.

Berkowitz, Marvin W. 2006. Fostering goodness: Teaching parents to facilitate children's moral development. http://parenthood.library.wisc.edu/Berkowitz/Berkowitz.html.

Berzin, C., Cauzinille-Marmeche E. & F. Winnykamen. 1995. Effet des interactions socials dans la resolution d'une tache de combinatoire aupres d'enfants de CM1 [The effect of social interaction on fourth grade students' solution of a combination task]. *Archives de psychologie*, 63(244):17-42.

Between the Lines. 2006. Interview with Antonio Damasio: Looking for Spinoza. http://www.harcourtbooks.com/authorinterviews/bookinterview_Damasio.asp.

Bleiker, C. A. 1999. The development of self through art: A case for early art education. *Art Education*, 52:48-53.

Bloomer, M. 2001. Young lives, learning and transformation: Some theoretical considerations. *Oxford Review of Education*, 27:429-449.

Bodrova, E., Leong, D. Norford, J. and D. Paynter. (n.d.). It only looks like child's play. *Journal of Staff Development*, 2(24):15-19.

Bodrova, Elena and Deborah J. Leong. 2003. The importance of being playful. *Educational Leadership*, 60, no.7 (April 2003):50-53.

Bounds, Christopher and L. Harrison. 1997. The brain-flex project. *Educational Leadership*, 55, no. 1 (September 1997):69-70.

Bowman, B., Donovan, M.S., & Burns, M.S. 2000. *Eager to learn: Educating our preschoolers.* Washington, DC: National Academies Press.

Brandt, Ron. 1993. On teaching for understanding: A conversation with Howard Gardner. *Educational Leadership* 50, no. 7 (1993): 4-7.

Bransford, J., Brown, A. & R. Cocking, R. eds. 2000. *How people learn: Brain, mind, experience, and school.* Washington, DC: National Research Council.

Bredekamp, S. & Rosegrant, T. 1994. Learning and teaching with technology. In J.L. Wright & D.D. Shade Eds. *Young children: Active learners in a technological age* (53-61). Washington, DC: National Association for the Education of Young Children.

Brooks, G. J. & M. G. Brooks. 1993. In search of understanding: The case for constructivist classrooms. Alexandria, VA: ASCD.

Brooks, J.B. 2004. To see beyond the lesson. *Educational Leadership*, 62, no. 1, (September 2004):8-13.

Brooks, M. G. and J.G. Brooks. 1999. The courage to be constructivist. *Educational Leadership*, no. 57 (November 1999)57:18-24.

Bruner, J.S. 1973. Beyond the information given: Studies in the psychology of knowing. New York: Norton.

—. 1971. The relevance of education. New York: Norton.

—. 1966. Toward a theory of instruction. New York: Norton.

Burns, Mary. 2005. Tools for the Mind. *Educational Leadership* 63, no. 4 (December 2005): 48-53.

Burts, D. Hart, C., R. Charlesworth, & L. Kirk. 1990. A comparison of frequencies of stress behaviors observed in kindergarten children in classrooms with developmentally appropriate versus developmentally inappropriate instructional practices. *Early Childhood Research Quarterly*, 5:407-423.

Burts, D., Hart C., R. Charlesworth, D. DeWolf, J. Ray, K. Manuel and P. Fleege. 1993. Developmental appropriateness of kindergarten programs and academic outcomes in first grade. *Journal of Research in Childhood Education*, 8(1):23-31.

Byrnes, D. A. 2001. Travel schooling: Helping children learn through travel. *Childhood Education* 77:345-355.

Campbell, Linda. 1997. Variations on a theme: How teachers interpret MI theory. *Educational Leadership* 55(1):14-19.

Cantrell, Mary Lou, S. A. Ebdon, R. Firlik, D. Johnson, and D. Rearick. 1997. The summer stars program. *Educational Leadership* 55, no. 1 (September 1997):38-42.

Charlton, Bruce G. 2006. Review of *The Feeling of What Happens: Body, Emotion and the Making of Consciousness* by Antonio Damasio. http://www.hedweb.com/bgcharlton/damasioreview.html.

Chuang, H. & Thompson. 2006. Students teaching teachers. *Educational Leadership* 63(4):70-71.

Checkley, Kathy. 1997. The first seven…and the eighth: A conversation with Howard Gardner. *Educational Leadership* 55, no. 1(September 1997):8-13.

Chen, M., Jane M. Healy; Mitchel J. Resnick, Laurie A. Lipper, Wendy Lazarus and Chris J. Dede. 2000. Looking to the future. *The Future of Children*, 10; 2:168-180.

Chinn, C.A. & Brewer, W.F. 1993. The role of anomalous data in knowledge acquisition: a theoretical framework and implications for science instruction. *Review of Educational Research* 63(1):1-49.

Christie, James F. & Enz, Billie. 1992. The effects of literacy play interventions on preschoolers' play patterns and literacy development. *Early Education and Development* 3(3): 205-220.

Clark, G. and E. Zimmerman. 1998. Nurturing the arts in programs for gifted and talented students. *Phi Delta Kappan* 79:747-752.

Clements, D. H., Nastasi, B.K., & Swaminathan, S. 1993. Young children and computers: Crossroads and directions from research. *Young Children* 48(2):56-64.

Clements, D. H. 1999. Young children and technology. Dialogue on early childhood science, mathematics, and technology education. Washington, DC: American Association for the Advancement of Science. http://www.project2061.org/newsinfo/earlychild/experience/clements.htm.
Cochrane, Cathy. 2004. Landscapes for learning. *Educational Leadership* 62, no. 1 (September 2004): 78-81.
Colburn, Alan. 2004. Inquiring scientists want to know. *Educational Leadership* 62, no. 1 (September 2004): 63-66.
Coles, Robert. 1997. *The moral intelligence of children.* New York: Penguin Putnam, Inc.
Cordes, Colleen and Edward. Miller, Eds. 2000. *Fool=s gold: A critical look at computers in childhood.* www.allianceforchildhood.net/projects/computers/computers_reports_fools_gold_contents .
Cornett, C. and Cornett, C. 1980. *Bibliotherapy: The right book at the right time.* Bloomington, Ind.: Phi Delta Kappa Education Foundation.
Corriveau, Kathleen H., Elisabeth S. Pasquini and Paul L. Harris. 2005. It's in your mind, it's in your knowledge@: Children's developing anatomy of identity. *Cognitive Development*, 186:1-20.
Cotton, K. 2006. Developing empathy in children and youth. *Northwest Regional Educational Laboratory.* http://www.nwrel.org/scpd/sirs/7/cul3.html.
Csikszentmihalyi, Mihaly, Abuhamdeh, S. & J. Nakamura. 2005. Flow. In Elliot, A. & Dweck, C.S., Eds. *Handbook of competence and motivation.* New York: Guilford Press.
Csikszentmihalyi, Mihaly. 1996. *Creativity: Flow and the psychology of discovery and invention.* New York: Harper-Collins.
—. 1988. Society, culture, and person: A systems view of creativity. In R. J. Sternberg, Ed., *The nature of creativity.* New York: Cambridge University Press, 325-339.
Damasio, Antonio. 1994. *Descartes' error: Emotion, reason, and the human brain.* New York: Grosset-Putnam and Harper Collins (1995).
—. 2003. *Looking for Spinoza: Joy, sorrow and the feeling brain.* New York: Harcourt Brace.
—. 1999. *The feeling of what happens: Body, emotion and the making of consciousness.* New York: Harcourt Brace.
DaSilva, E. & Winnykamen, F. 1998. Degree of sociability and interactive behaviors in dyadic situations of problem solving. *European Journal of Psychology of Education* 13(2):253-270.

Davidson, J. & Wright, J.L. 1994. The potential of the microcomputer in the early childhood classroom. In J. L. Wright & D.D. Shade Eds. *Young children: Active learners in a technological age* (77-91). Washington, DC: National Association for the Education of Young Children.

Davilla, Donna E. & Koenig, Susan M. 1998. Bringing the Reggio concept to American educators. *Art Education* 51, no 4(1998):18-24.

Davis, B.C. & Shade, D.D. 1994. *Integrate, don't isolate! Computers in the early childhood curriculum.* ERIC Digest. Urbana IL: ERIC Clearinghouse on Elementary and Early Childhood Education.

Dede, Chris, Clarke, Jody, Ketelhut, Diane J., Brian Nelson and Cassie Bowman. 2005. *Students' motivation and learning of science in a multi-user virtual environment.* Paper presented at AERA. http://muve.gse.harvard.edu/rivercityproject/prior_research/research.html.

DePillis, Lydia. 2004. Taking technology to Takoradi. *Educational Leadership* 63, no. 4 (December 2005): 80-84.

DeVries, Rheta and Betty Zan. (2003). When children make rules. *Educational Leadership* 61, no. 1(September 2003) 64-67.

Dewey, J., 1911. *Moral principles in education.* Boston: Houghton Mifflin.

—. 1964. The relation of theory to practice in education. In R. Arcahmault (Ed.), *John Dewey on Education: Selected Writings.* New York: Random House, 313-338.

Dunn, L., Beach, S. & S. Kontos. 1994. Quality of the literacy environment in day care and children's development. *Journal of Research in Childhood Education,* 9(1):24-34.

Durkheim, Emile. 1925(1961). *Moral education.* Glencoe, Ill: Free Press.

Edutopia Online. 2006. Daniel Goleman on Emotional Intelligence. The George Lucas Foundation. www.glef.org.

Einarsdottir, Johanna. 2000. Incorporating literacy resources into the play curriculum of two Icelandic preschools. In Kathleen A. Roskos & James F. Christie, Eds. *Play and literacy in early childhood: Research from multiple perspectives* (77-90).

Eisner, Elliot. 2005. Back to whole. *Educational Leadership,* 63 no. 1 (September 2005):14-18.

Elliott, Julian and Neil Hufton, Leonid Illushin, and Fraser Lauchlan. 2003. Motivation in the junior years: International perspectives on children's attitudes, expectations and behaviour and their relationship to educational achievement. *Oxford Review of Education,* 27:37-68.

El-Sheikh Hasan. O.H. 2000. Improving the quality of learning: Global education as a vehicle for school reform. *Theory into Practice* 39:97-103.

Ewing Marion Kauffman Foundation. 2002. *Set for success: Building a strong foundation for school readiness based on the social-emotional development of young children.* Kansas City, MO: Author.

Feldman, David Henry and Goldsmith, L. 1991. *Nature's gambit: Child prodigies and the development of human potential.* New York: Teachers College Press.

Ferrero, David J. 2006. Having it all. *Educational Leadership* 63, no.8 (May 2006):8-15.

Fischer, K. W. 1980. A theory of cognitive development: The control and construction of hierarchies of skills. *Psychological Review* 87:477-531.

Fischer, K.W., Rotenberg, E.J., Bullock, D.H. and P. Raya. 1993. The dynamics of competence. How context contributes directly to skill. In R.H. Wozniak & K.W. Fischer, Eds. *Development in context: Acting and thinking in specific environments.* The Jean Piaget Symposium Series. Hillsdale, NJ: Erlbaum, 93-17.

Fischer, K.W., Shaver, P.R. and P. Carnochan 1990. How emotions develop and how they organize development. *Cognition and Emotion* 4(2):81-127.

Fisher, Edward P. 1992. The impact of play on development: A meta-analysis. *Play and Culture* 5(2), 159-181.

Frede, E. & Barnett, W.S. 1992. Developmentally appropriate public school preschool: A study of implementation of the high/scope curriculum and its effects on disadvantaged children's skills at first grade. *Early Childhood Research Quarterly* 7: 483-499.

Freeman, John G., Jean C. McPhail and Julie A. Berndt. 2002. Sixth graders' views of activities that do and do not help them learn. *The Elementary School Journal 102:*335-347.

Freud, S. 1989. Creative writers and day-dreaming. In P. Gay, Ed., *The Freud reader.* New York: Norton, 436-443. (Original work published 1907).

Gardner, Howard. 1982. *Art, mind and brain: A cognitive approach to creativity.* New York: Basic Books.

—. 1991. Making schools more like museums. *Education Week* 11(5):10.

—. 1997. Multiple intelligences as a partner in school improvement. *Educational Leadership* 55, no. 1(September 1997): 20-21.

—. 1993. *Multiple intelligences: The theory in practice.* New York: Basic Books.

—. 1999. *The disciplined mind: What all students should understand.* New York: Simon & Shuster.

Gartenhaus, A. 1991. *Minds in motion: Using museums to expand creative thinking.* Davis, CA: Caddo Gap Press.

Glasersfeld, E. von. 1989. Constructivism in education. In T. Husen & N. Postlethwaite, Eds. *International Encyclopedia in Education,* Supplementary Volume. Oxford: Pergamon.

Goodlad, J. I. 1977. What goes on in our schools? *Educational Researcher* 6:3-6.

Goodlad, J. I. 1979. *What schools are for.* Bloomington, IN: Phi Delta Kappa Educational Foundation.

Greenhawk, Jan. 1997. Multiple intelligences meet standards. *Educational Leadership* 55(1):62-64.

Grigorenko, E. L., Jarvin, L. & R. J. Sternberg. 2002. School-based tests of the triarchic theory of intelligence: Three settings, three samples, three syllabi. *Contemporary Educational Psychology* 27:167-208.

Hartshorne, H. and M.A. May, 1928-30. *Studies in the nature of character* (3 vols.). New York: Macmillan.

Haugland, S.W. & Shade, D.D. 1994. Software evaluation for young children. In J.L. Wright & D.D. Shade Eds. *Young children: Active learners in a technological age* (66-76). Washington, DC: National Association for the Education of Young Children.

Haughland, S.W. 1992. The effect of computer software on preschool children's developmental gains. *Journal of Computing in Childhood Education* 3(1):15-30.

Healy, J.M. 1999. *Failure to connect: How computers affect our children's minds and what we can do about it.* New York: Simon & Shuster/Touchstone.

Healy, J.M. 1998. Understanding TV's effect on the developing brain. *AAP News: The Official News Magazine of the American Academy of Pediatrics.* http://www.aap.org.advocacy/chm98nws.htm

Hedges, H. 2004. A whale of an interest in sea creatures: The learning potential of excursions. *Early Childhood Research and Practice* 6:NA.

Helm, Judy Harris. 2004. Projects that power young minds. *Educational Leadership* 62, no. 1 (September 2004): 58-62.

Henderson, L. M., and F. Ebner. 1997. The biological basis for early intervention with gifted children. *Peabody Journal of Education,* Parts 1 and 2:59-80.

Hoerr, Thomas R. 1997. Frog ballets and musical fractions. *Educational Leadership* 55, no. 1 (September 1997): 43-46.

Hyson, M. Hirsh-Pasek, K. & L. Rescorla. 1990. The classroom practices inventory: An observation instrument based on NAEYC's guidelines for developmentally appropriate practices for 4-and5-year old children. *Early Childhood Research Quarterly* 5:475-494.

Key Learning Community. 2006. Indianapolis, Indiana, http://www.616.ips.k12.in.us

Kim, Sook--Yi. 1999. The effects of storytelling and pretend play on cognitive processes, short-term and long-term narrative recall. *Child Study Journal* 29(3):175-191.

King, Rosalyn M. 2004. New WorldQuest: A game to promote global understanding and build a world community. Copyrighted April 2004, United States Copyright Office.

—.1992. Class, culture and learning. In *The audience in exhibition development*. Washington, DC: The American Association of Museums, w992.

Kohlberg, L. 1966. Moral education in the schools: A developmental view. *The School Review*, 74:1-30.

Knodt, Jean Sausele. 1997. A think tank cultivates kids. *Educational Leadership* 55, no. 1 (September 1997): 35-37.

Lambert, Wendy Ecklund. (1997). From Crockett to Tubman: Investigating historical perspectives. *Educational Leadership*, 55, no. 1 (September 1997): 51-57.

Lehrer, R, M. Lee, and A. Jeong. 1999. Reflective teaching of Logo. *The Journal of the Learning Sciences* 8:245-289.

Lewis, C.S. 1947. The abolition of man. New York: Macmillan.

Lickona, T. 2006. Center for the 4th & 5th Rs: Respect & Responsibility. http://www.cortland.edu/character.

—. 1993. The return of character education. *Educational Leadership* 51, no 3 (November 1993):6-11.

McTighe, Jay, Elliott Seif and Grant Wiggins. 2004. You can teach for meaning. *Educational Leadership* 62, no. 1 (September 2004): 26-30.

Melson, G. 2006. Robotic pets and children. http://www.ischool.washington.edu/vsd/projects/aibodevelopmental.html (accessed January 2006).

Merrefield, Gayle E. 1997. Three Billy goats and Gardner. *Educational Leadership* 55, no. 1 (September 1997): 58-61.

Meyer, Maggie. 1997. The greening of learning: Using the eighth intelligence. *Educational Leadership* 55, no. 1 (September 1997): 32-34.

Moran, Seana and John-Steiner, Vera. 2003. Creativity in the Making: Vygotsky's Contemporary Contribution to the Dialectic of development and Creativity. In Sawyer, R., John-Steiner, V., S. Moran, R.J. Sternberg, D. H. Feldman, J. Nakamura, and M. Csikszentmihalyi. *Creativity and Development.* Oxford: Oxford University Press, 61-90.

Neuman, Susan B. & Roskos, Kathy. 1992. Literacy objects as cultural tools: Effects on children's literacy behaviors in play. *Reading Research Quarterly* 27(3):202-225.

New, Rebecca. 2000. Reggio Emilia: Catalyst for Change and Conversation. *ERIC Digest.* ED447971. http://www.ericdigests.org/1993/reggio.htm.

—. 1993. Reggio Emilia: Some lessons for U.S. Educators. *ERIC Digest.* ED354988. http://www.ericdigests.org/1993/reggio.htm.

Newmann, Fred. M., Helen M. Marks, and Adam Gamoran. 1996). Authentic pedagogy and student performance. *American Journal of Education* 104, no.4 (1996):280-312.

Newman, Fred M. and Gary G. Wehlage. 1993. Five standards of authentic instruction. *Educational Leadership* 50, no 7 (April 1993): 8-12.

Noddings, N. 2005. What does it mean to educate the whole child? *Educational Leadership,* 63, no. 1 (September 2005):8-13.

Novick, R. 1998. *Learning to read and write: A place to start.* Portland, OR: Northwest Regional Educational Laboratory. http://www.nwrel.org/cfc/publications/learningreadwrite.html.

Palmer, Parker. J. 1997. *The courage to teach: Exploring the inner landscape of a teacher's life.* New Jersey: Jossey-Bass.

Perkins, David. 2004. Knowledge alive. *Educational Leadership,* 62, no. 1 (September 2004):14-18.

Piaget, J. 1962. Play, dreams, and imitation in childhood. New York: Norton.

Piaget, Jean. 1932. The moral judgment of the child.

Puustinen, M. & Winnykamen, F. 1998. Influence du sentiment d'auto-efficacité dans la demande d'aide chez des enfants de 8 á 9 ans [The effect of the feeling of self-efficacy on 8-9 year olds' help-seeking behavior]. *Enfance* 2:173-188.

Ohler, Jason. (2006). *Digital stories in the classroom: A telling experience.* Corwin Press.

—. (2005). The world of digital storytelling. *Educational Leadership* 63, no. 4 (December 2005): 44-47.

Ragozzino, K., Resnik, H., M. Utne-O'Brien & R. P. Weissberg. 2003. *Horizons (Quarterly Journal of Pi Lambda Theta,* Inc., Bloomington, IN). Summer 2003:169-171.

Ramey-Gassert, L. 1997. Learning science beyond the classroom. *The Elementary School Journal* 97:433-450.

Ravitch, D. (2003). A nation at risk: Twenty years later. Weekly Essay: Hoover Institution. http://www-hoover.stanford.edu/pubaffairs/we/2003/ravitch04.html (accessed May 9, 2006).

Reid, Carol and Brenda Romanoff. 1997. Using multiple intelligence theory to identify gifted children. *Educational Leadership* 55, no. 1 (September 1997): 71-75.

Renshaw, P.D. 1992. The sociocultural theory of teaching and learning: implications for the curriculum in the Australian context. Paper presented at the Annual Conference of the Australian Association for Research in Education. Deakin University, Geelong, Victoria.

Renzulli, Joseph S., Marcia Gentry, and Sally M. Reis. 2004. A time and a place for authentic learning. *Educational Leadership* 62, no.1 (September 2004): 73-77.

Resnick, Mitchel J. 2000. Commentary 3. In M. Chen, J.M. Healy, M. Resnick, L. Lipper, W. Lazarus & C. Dede. *The Future of Children* 10(2), Children and Computer Technology: 168-180.

Roberts, D.F., Foehr, U.G., Rideout, V.J. & M. Brodie. 1999. *Kids and media @ the new millennium.* Menlo Park, CA: Henry J. Kaiser Family Foundation. http://www.kff.org/content/a999/1535/KidsReport%.

Rogoff, B. 1998. Cognition as a collaborative process. In D. Kuhn & R.S. Siegler Eds. Handbook of Child Psychology: Volume 2. Cognition, perception, and language. New York: Wiley, 679-744.

Roschelle, Jeremy M., Roy D. Pea, Christopher M. Hoadley, Douglas N. Gordin and Barbara M. Means. Changing how and what children learn in school with computer-based technologies. *The Future of Children,* 10: 76-101.

Roskos, K. & Christie, J.F. Eds. 2000. Play and literacy in early childhood: Research from multiple perspectives. Mahwah, NJ: Erlbaum.

Rushton, Stephen and Elizabeth Larkin. 2001. Shaping the learning environment: Connecting developmentally appropriate practices to brain research. *Early Childhood Education Journal,* 29, no.1 (2001): 25-33.

Ryan, K.1993. Mining the values in the curriculum. *Educational Leadership* 5, no. 3 (November 1993)1:16-18.

Sawyer, R. Keith, Vera John-Steiner, Seana Moran, Robert J. Sternberg, David Henry Feldman, Jeanne Nakamura and Mihaly Csikszentmihalyi.

2003. *Creativity and Development.* Oxford: Oxford University Press.
Sawyer, R. K. 1997. *Pretend play as improvisation: Conversation in the preschool classroom.* Mahwah, NJ: Erlbaum.
Scherer, Marge. 2002. Do students care about learning? A conversation with Mihaly Csikszentmihalyi. *Educational Leadership* 60, no.1 (September 2002):142-145.
—. 2004. Perspectives: I had this teacher. *Educational Leadership,* 62, no.1 (September 2004):7-7.
—. 2006. Perspectives: The challenge to change. Educational Leadership, 63, no8 (May 2006): 7-7.
Schiller, F. 1968. On the aesthetic education of man, in a series of letters (E.M. Wilkinson & L.A. Willoughby, Eds. and Trans.) Oxford, UK: Clarendon Press.
Scoter, J.V., D. Ellis and J. Railsback. 2001. Technology in Early childhood Education: Finding the Balance. *Northwest Regional Educational Laboratory.* http://nwrel.org/request/june01/textonly.html. (Accessed January 2006).
Sherman, Thomas M. and Barbara L. Kurshan. 2005. Constructing learning: Using technology to support teaching for understanding. *Learning and Leading with Technology* 32:105-109.
Shonkoff, J.P. & Phillips, D.A. Eds. 2000. *From neurons to neighborhoods: The science of early childhood development.* Washington, DC: National Academies Press.
Siegler, R.S. 2000. The rebirth of children's learning. *Child Development,* 71:26-35.
Sisk, D.A. 1982. Caring and sharing: Moral development of gifted students. *The Elementary School Journal,* 82: 221-229.
Sivin-Kachala, J. & Bialo, E.R. 1994. Report on the effectiveness of technology in schools, 1990-1994. Washington, DC: Software Publishers Association. (ERIC Document Reproduction Service No. ED 371 726.
Smilansky, S. & Shefatya, L. 1990. *Facilitating play: A medium for promoting cognitive, socio- emotional, and academic development in young children.* Gaithersburg, MD: Psychological and educational Publications.
Smolucha, L.W., & Smolucha, F. C. 1986. L.S. Vygotsky's theory of creative imagination. *SPIEL,* 5(2), 299-308. Frankfurt, Germany: Verlag Peter Lang.
Spodek, B. 1971. Alternatives to traditional education. *Peabody Journal of Education* 48: 140-146.

Stan, S. 1999. Going global: World literature for American children. *Theory into Practice* 38:168-177.
Sternberg, Robert J. 2003. The development of creativity as a decision-making process. In Sawyer, R., John-Steiner, V., S. Moran, R.J. Sternberg, D. H. Feldman, J. Nakamura and M. Csikszentmihalyi. *Creativity and Development.* Oxford: Oxford University Press, 91-138.
Stone, Sandra J. & Christie, James F. 1996. Collaborative literacy learning during sociodramatic play in a multiage (K-2) primary classroom. *Journal of Research in Childhood Education* 10(2): 123-133.
Subotnik, R. F. and P. Olszewski-Kubilius. 1997. Restructuring special programs to reflect the distinctions between children's and adults' experiences with giftedness. *Peabody Journal of Education:* 72:101-116.
Suizzo, Marie-Anne. 2000. The social-emotional and cultural contexts of cognitive development: Neo-Piagetian perspectives. *Child Development*, 71:846-849.
Swezy, Shanta. 1997. An American in Kazakhstan: Life in a fish bowl. *Educational Leadership* 55, no.1 (September 1997): 80-83.
Tell, C. 2000. The I-generation-from toddlers to teenagers: A conversation with Jane M. Healy. *Educational Leadership* 58:8-13.
Tomlinson, Carol. 1995. *How to differentiate instruction in mixed-ability classrooms.* Alexandria, VA: Association for Supervision and Curriculum Development.
—. 2005. *Differentiating instruction for advanced learners in the mixed-ability middle school classroom.*
http://www.kidsource.com/kidsource/content/diff_instruction.html.
The Collaborative for Academic, Social, and Emotional Learning (CASEL). 2006. www.CASEL.org.
Verba, M. & Winnykamen, F. 1992. Expert-novice interactions: Influence of partner status. *European Journal of Psychology of Education* 7(1):61-71.
Vialle, Wilma. 1997. Multiple intelligences in multiple settings. *Educational Leadership* 55, no.1 (September 1997): 65-68.
Vygotsky, L.S. 1987. Emotions and their development in childhood. In R.W. Rieber & A.S.Carton, Eds. *The collected works of L.S. Vygotsky* (Vol. 1, N. Minick Trans., 325-338). New York: Plenum Press. (Original work published in *Voprosy Psikhologii*, 3, 1959).
—. 1998. Imagination and creativity in the adolescent. In R.W. Rieber, Ed. *The collected works of L. S. Vygotsky* (Vol.5, M. J. Hall, Trans., 151-166). New York: Plenum Press. (Original work published in

Pedologija podrostka, Moscow: Izd-voBZO pri Pedfake 2-go MGU, 1931).
—. 1997a. Mind, consciousness, the unconscious. In R. W. Rieber & J. Wollock, Eds., *The collected works of L.S. Vygotsky* (Vol. 3, R. Van der Veer, Trans., 109-122). New York: Plenum Press. (Original work published in *Elementy obshschej psikhologii,* 48-61, Moscow: Isdatelstvo BZO pri Pedfake 2-go MGU, 1930.
—. 1978. *Mind in society: The development of higher psychological processes.* M. Cole, V. John-Steiner, S. Scriber, & E. Souberman, Eds. Cambridge, MA: Harvard University Press.
—. 1997b. The history of the development of higher mental functions. In R.W. Rieber, Ed. *The collected works of L.S. Vygotsky* (Vol.4, M. J. Hall, Trans., 1-251). New York: Plenum Press. (Original work published as Razvite vysshikh psikhicheskikh funktsii, Moscow, 1960).
—. 1999. Tool and sign in the development of the child. In R.W. Rieber, Ed., *The collected works of L. S. Vygotsky* (Vol. 6, M. J. Hall, Trans, 1068.) New York: Kluwer Academic/Plenum Press. (Original work published in *Sobr. Soch. V6-ti-t, Vol. 6,* 5-90, Moscow: Pedagogika, 1984).
Wang, M. C., G.D. Haertel and H.J. Walberg, 1997. Learning influences. In H.J. Walberg & G.D. Haertel, Eds. *Psychology and Educational Practice.* Berkeley, CA: McCutchan.
White, P. 1999. Political education in the early years: The place of civic virtues. *Oxford Review of Education* 25:59-70.
Willard-Holt, Colleen. 2003. Raising expectations for the gifted. *Educational Leadership* 61, no. 2 (October 2003): 72-75.
Wilson, D.B., Gottfredson, D.C. & S.S. Najaka. 2001. School-based prevention of problem behaviors: A meta-analysis. Journal of Quantitative Criminology 17:247-272.
Wikipedia. 2006. Reggio Emilia approach. http://en.wikipedia.org/wiki/Reggio_Emilia_approach.
Wiske, Stone. 2004. Using technology to dig for meaning. *Educational Leadership* 62, no. 1 (September 2004): 46-50.
Woolfolk, Anita. 2001. Educational Psychology. Boston: Allyn & Bacon.
Wyver, Shirley R. & Spence, Susan H. 1999. Play and divergent problem-solving: Evidence supporting a reciprocal relationship. *Early Education and Development* 10(4):419-444.
Zorman, R. 1997. Eureka: the cross-cultural model for identification of hidden talent through enrichment. *Roeper Review* 20:54-62.

Zhao, Yang. 2006. Are we fixing the wrong things? *Educational Leadership* 63, no. 8 (May 2006):28-31.

Zins, J.E., Weissberg, R.P., M.L. Wang, & H.J. Walberg, eds. (In Press in 2003). *Building school success through social and emotional learning: Implications for practice and research.* New York: Teachers College.

Zull, James E. 2004. The art of changing the brain. *Educational Leadership* 62, no. 1 (September 2004): 68-72.

APPENDICES

APPENDIX A

CHARACTER EDUCATION PARTNERSHIP

100 Ways to Promote Character Education
Value of the Month

Examples of Character School Program Models
—Shaping Character through Children's Literature
—Participatory School Democracy
—The Sweet Home Story
—The Child Development Project

100 Ways to Promote Character Education

1. Hang pictures of heroes and heroines in halls and classrooms.
2. Institute a student-tutoring program.
3. Promote service clubs with real missions for the school community.
4. Be vigilant about preventing and stopping scapegoating of one child by other children.
5. Create recognition programs that acknowledge something besides academic, athletics, or artistic achievement.
6. Seriously and thoughtfully grade student behavior and contribution to the community.
7. Create a code of behavior for your classroom (and school) to which students and teacher agree.
8. Invite parents to observe and contribute to your classroom.
9. Choose a personal motto and share it with your students.
10. Promote a "virtue of the month;" study it.
11. Share a personal hero and tell the students why he or she is your hero.
12. Regularly weave into your discussion of stories and history and other subjects asking, "what's the right thing to do?" and follow up with a discussion.
13. Help students to see that the "good" in students is more than academic success.
14. Treat ethical issues like other intellectual issues—get the facts, gather evidence, weigh consequences, and make a decision.
15. Structure opportunities for your students to do service in the community.
16. Lead by example. For instance, pick up the discarded piece of paper in the hall. Clean the chalkboard out of respect for the next teacher.
17. Don't allow unkindness of any kind in your classroom.
18. Do not permit swearing, vulgar or obscene language in classrooms or anywhere on school property.
19. Involve parents in student misbehavior through notes, calls, visits.
20. Write, call, or visit parents to praise their children.
21. Make it clear that students have a moral responsibility to work hard in school.
22. Use ethical language with faculty colleagues… "I have a responsibility to…," "the courage of her conviction caused her to…," "my neglect led

him to...."
23. Include the study of "local heroes" in your social studies classes.
24. Institute an honor system for test-taking and homework assignments.
25. Create a charity. Collect donations and have the students decide on their distribution.
26. Reinforce the moral authority of parents, urging students to take their moral problems to their parents. Discuss with students why this is sometimes difficult.
27. Have sayings on the wall that encourage good character, such as "don't wait to be a great person: start now!"
28. Share stories of ethical conflict, especially ones involving students in their present setting. Don't hesitate to write it and have them struggle to put their views on paper.
29. Celebrate birthdays of heroes and heroines with observance and/or discussion of their accomplishments.
30. Have students write their own sayings of significance and display on walls.
31. Reward students for bringing in articles about ethics and moral issues. Use them in class discussion.
32. Discuss campus "issues of character" on a regular basis (vandalism, good deeds, etc.)
33. Make classroom expectations clear, and hold students accountable for them.
34. Strive to be consistent in dealings with students; avoid allowing personal feelings to interfere with fairness.
35. Admit mistakes and seek to correct them. Expect and encourage students to do the same.
36. Read aloud a "Two-Minute Story" everyday to begin or end the school day. Choose stories that are brief, yet value-centered.
37. Consider ethical implications when establishing classroom and school policies and procedures; be aware of what messages they send to students.
38. Explain the reasons for a particular school or classroom policy, action, or decision. Help students to understand "why," not just "what."
39. Have students discuss the ethical and character-developing elements of being a good student.
40. Teach your students about competition, helping them to see when it is valuable and when it is not.
41. Talk to your students about why you are a teacher. Explain how you

understand the importance and responsibility of teaching.

42. Let your students know about your community service. Tell them about volunteering in a food bank, coaching Little League, or teaching religion at your temple or church.

43. Teach students to analyze the media critically. To what extent do their messages encourage living a life of character.

44. Bring recent high school graduates back to talk about their successful transitions to college, work, or the military.

45. Invite local adults to talk about how they have integrated the concept of character into their adult lives.

46. Help reinforce student's empathy. Ask them questions like "how would you feel if no one would play with you?" or, "how would you feel if someone made fun of your name because they thought that it was strange sounding?

47. When conflicts arise at school, teach students the importance of respect, open-mindedness, privacy, and discretion. Do not allow conversations that are fueled by gossip or disrespect.

48. Overtly teach courtesy. Teach students how to listen attentively to other students and adults, and to avoid interrupting people.

49. Read and discuss biographies of accomplished individuals. For students in upper grades, encourage them to be discerning, seeing that an individual may have flaws but still be capable of much admirable action.

50. Assign older students to assist younger ones, such as seniors paired with freshmen, to show them the school.

51. Emphasize from the first day of class the importance of working hard and striving for certain standards of achievement.

52. Encourage high school students to become more active in their community by attending city, town, or school board meetings.

53. During the election season, encourage students to research candidates' positions.

54. Encourage high school students to volunteer for voter registration drives, and, if eligible, to vote.

55. Teach students how to write thank-you notes. As a class, write thank-you notes to people who have done thoughtful things for the students.

56. Give students sufficient feedback when evaluating their work. Demonstrate to students that you are making an effort to communicate to them how they are succeeding and how they can improve.

57. Have older students sponsor a potluck supper for their parents. Have

students cook, decorate and clean-up.

58. Begin a monthly "gift-giving" from your class. Have the class perform some service to the school, such as decorating a hallway.

59. Work together as a class or school to clean classrooms or school grounds on a regular basis.

60. Demonstrate your respect for other religions and cultures. Talk to students about the moral imperative to act justly towards others.

61. Stand up for the "underdog" when he or she is being treated unfairly. Use this as a teaching moment.

62. Have children in self-contained classrooms take turns caring for their class pets, taking them home on weekends or holidays. Talk to them about the need to care for other living creatures.

63. Start or expand a class or school recycling program. Talk about the general principles of carefully using what you have, and not wasting.

64. Highlight certain programs in your school such as SADD or the National Honor Society, which may already be emphasizing character.

65. Have students volunteer to clean up their community. With parental support, encourage students to build a community playground, pick up litter, rake leaves, grow plants, paint a mural on the side of a building, or clean up a local beach.

66. Dust off the school song (alma mater). Teach students, especially the newest ones, the words, talk about their meaning, and include it in every school activity.

67. If your school doesn't have a school song, sponsor some sort of contest for students to write one. As a school community, talk about what kinds of ideas should be included in that song.

68. Emphasize and teach the significance of school rituals. Talk about the importance of recognizing certain rights as a community and properly acknowledging them.

69. Encourage students to look in on elderly or sick neighbors, particularly during harsh winter months.

70. Start a pen pal exchange between your students and students from a distant sate or country. Share the information your students learn about their pen pals' lives. Encourage discussion about how life must be like living in that community.

71. Use the curriculum to teach character. For example, in language arts class, have student assume a character's point of view and write about it. Regularly ask questions requiring students to "walk in someone else's shoes."

72. Use constructive criticism, tempered by compassion. Help students do the same with each other.

73. Emphasize good sportsmanship in sports, games, and daily interactions with others.

74. When making school policy, allow students' participation and responsibility in some decisions. Have them research the various ramifications of different policies and present their findings to the administrators and faculty for decisions.

75. Collect interesting, thought-provoking quotes worthy of reflection, discussion, and writing—such as "the truth never becomes clear as long as we assume that each one of us, individually is the center of the universe." (Thomas Merton). Ask students to do the same.

76. Develop a list of suggested readings in character education that teachers and administrators can use as resources.

77. Develop a school motto.

78. Institute a character honor roll.

79. Foster the development of students' self-esteem by providing opportunities for genuine academic and social challenge and achievement.

80. Include in faculty/staff meetings and workshops discussions of the schools "moral climate," and the desired goals for the moral life of the school.

81. Develop a "School Code of Ethics." Refer to it in all school activity and policy. Disseminate it to all school member. Display it prominently throughout the building.

82. Begin an "exchange network" or "bulletin board" by which teachers and administrators can share their own "100 Ways to Promote Character Education."

83. Include anecdotes of commendable student behavior in the school newsletter to parents.

84. Start a school scrapbook with photos, news stories, and memorabilia reflecting the school's history and accomplishments. Include all school members in contributing to and maintaining the collection. Show it off to school visitors.

85. Publicly recognize the work and achievement of the school's "unsung heroes"—the custodians, repairmen, secretaries, cafeteria workers and volunteers—who keep things running everyday.

86. Assign reasonable amounts of homework that stimulate and challenge students while teaching the importance of self-discipline and perseverance in learning.

87. Design a school pledge that students recite weekly. Include it in school documents, especially those intended for parents.

88. Institute a dress code, explaining its role in promoting an educational environment conducive to learning, but always emphasize the importance of individuality.

89. Use homeroom periods for activities that develop school community and cohesion among students, and a sense of attachment to their school.

90. Create opportunities for parents and students to work together on a school project: for example, a dance, symposium, dinner, or field trip.

91. Be attentive to the physical appearance of the building. Involve all school members in the shared responsibility of general cleanliness and order.

92. Seek ways to involve local businesses in the life of the school, perhaps through mentoring opportunities or partnerships with student groups.

93. Establish a newcomers' club for newly hired personnel and entering students.

94. Invite local employers to talk to students about the importance of good moral character in the world of work.

95. Have athletes and coaches collaborate to develop a code of ethics for athletics.

96. Sponsor a public forum on character education in your community.

97. Ask each school organization to design a logo symbolizing a character trait representative of the club's mission.

98. Provide a bimonthly occasion for teachers to gather with their colleagues and study a text of literature, history philosophy, or other subject area that bears on ethics.

99. Develop for parents a bibliography of books that they can read with their children to stimulate conversation about good character.

100. Sponsor an after-school reading club for students, with age-appropriate literature focused on enduring moral lessons.

This list was compiled by the staff of the Center for the Advancement of Ethics and Character at Boston University with the input from numerous teachers and administrators. Boston University, Center for the Advancement of Ethics and Character, 605 Commonwealth Avenue, Boston, MA 02212; Ph (617) 353-3262. Available online at: http://www.cortland.edu/character/articles.htm.

Example 1 of Character Education Model

Value of the Month

Carl Campbell is principal at Dry Creek Elementary School in Clovis, California. He explains that the school's mission is to help students develop their potential in five areas:

1. academics
2. athletics
3. performing arts
4. citizenship in the school
5. citizenship in the community

And that commitment, he says, goes for every student:

> "Our philosophy is that we do everything we can do while we've got a kid. When he walks through that door, we're responsible for the quality of his experience. We may not be able to control his environment elsewhere, but we can control the environment here."

Dry Creek has a Value of the Month program: For an entire month, the whole school every teacher at every grade level focuses on the same value (e.g., honesty, cooperation, self-control, ambition).

Teachers talk to their students about the value of the month making connections, for example, with classroom incidents that arise. They work it into the writing assignments. They do special projects and displays related to the value. Students also bring in books or articles that tell about a person or incident that exemplifies the value.

Teachers take heart from the fact that they are all working together on a common value, something that is becoming part of the shared moral vocabulary that defines the common moral culture of their school.

Principal Campbell spoke about the impact this Value of the Month program had in a previous district where he worked:

> Before coming to Clovis, I was principal in a school where stealing was an everyday occurrence when I first arrived. The attitude among students was that it was okay to steal as long as you didn't get caught. There was

also a problem of kids being intimidated for their lunch money. I said to the faculty, "How can we change this?" We selected basic values to teach, one each month. We started with honesty. As time went on, kids started turning in money they found on the playground. Intimidation became less and less a problem. By the end of our second year with the program, stealing was a very rare event at this school.

Dry Creek Elemenatry School, 8098 North Armstrong, Clovis, CA 93611; (209) 299-2161.

Source: **Center for the 4th & 5th Rs: Respect and Responsibility.** Online: http://www.cortland.edu/character/success/success03.htm.

Example 2 of Character Education Model
Shaping Character through Children's Literature

The award winning- Heartwood Ethics Curriculum for children uses multicultural children's literature to foster seven character qualities affirmed by cultures around the world: courage, loyalty, justice, respect, hope, honesty, and love.

For each of these seven qualities, the Heartwood program provides six children's books (folk tales, hero stories, legends, and modern classics) along with interdisciplinary activities that develop children's understanding of the particular character quality and how to apply it.

Diane Root, a second-grade teacher using the Heartwood curriculum, tells of a mother who came to her and said, "What in the world are you doing this year at school? David is a different child." Her son David had previously often been in trouble in the classroom, on the bus, on the playground.

His teacher responded, "The only thing that's different is the Heartwood program. "She explained that when the class finishes studying a particular character attribute, one assignment is to go to the classroom mirror, stand in front, and ask themselves if they have shown that attribute (e.g., "Have I shown courage?". "Am I a respectful person?").
Then the child goes to his or her Heartwood Journal and writes a personal answer to that question. This encourages children to act upon the ethical insights emerging from their reading and discussion.

"Perhaps," the teacher concluded her conversation with the mother," when David looked in the classroom mirror, he decided to change."

Contact: The Heartwood Institute, 425 N. Craig Street, Suite 302, Pittsburgh, PA 15213; (412) 688-8570.

Source: **Center for the 4th & 5th Rs: Respect and Responsibility**. Online: http://www.cortland.edu/character/success/success08.htm.

Example 3 of Character Education Model

Participatory School Democracy

At Theodore Roosevelt Elementary School in Binghamton, New York, teacher Mary Ann Taylor decided to tackle the problem of her school cafeteria. She described the cafeteria as a "war zone" where teacher aides yelled at children, students yelled at each other, food fights were common, and the place was a mess when students left.

Teacher Taylor set up a Cafeteria Council with elected student delegates from each classroom.

At every grade level, classes held discussions: What are the characteristics of an ideal cafeteria? What should be the rules for cafeteria manners?

Delegates carried their classes' views into the Cafeteria Council's weekly meetings, where they discussed these ideas under the guidance of teacher Taylor and the school's principal and shaped them into action proposals.

The Council also conducted a survey of all students, staff, and parents on how to improve the cafeteria. It also solicited ideas on an ongoing basis through a Suggestion Box. It published a monthly newsletter reporting progress.

The positive outcomes of all this effort were many: Student cafeteria behavior improved greatly; students were enthusiastic about improvements in the cafeteria; parent feedback was very positive; a recycling project was begun; and, most important, the school decided to keep its new delegate system of democratic student government as a way to deal with other problems in the school environment, such as fights on the playground or bad behavior on the school bus.

Contact: Mary Ann Taylor, Theodore Roosevelt Elementary School, 9 Ogden Street, Binghamton, NY 13901; (607) 762-8283.

Source: **Center for the 4th & 5th Rs: Respect and Responsibility.** Online: http://www.cortland.edu/character/success/success09.htm.

Example 4 of Character Education Model
The Sweet Home Story

A District-wide Approach. In 1988 Dr. James Finch, then superintendent of Sweet Home Schools in Amherst, New York, wrote a letter to all district staff asking three questions: "Are you concerned about the values and attitudes of our students? Should the school be doing something about this? If so, would you like to be involved?"

Seventy-five persons wrote replies. Dr. Finch set up a 19-member District Values Education Council, chaired by Middle School teacher Sharon Banas and representing teachers, parents, administrators, paraprofessionals, classified personnel, students, and the School Board. The District Council then charged each building with the task of identifying its top values concerns and coming up with strategies for addressing them.

The building character education committees have continued the approach of getting everyone involved. Building committees have included administrators, teachers, librarians, nurses, secretaries, custodians, guidance counselors, parents, and students. Once a month representatives from each building meet to report activities they have successfully implemented in their schools. A monthly Values Education Newsletter describing these activities goes to all staff and parents.

At Sweet Home Middle School, students have made large vinyl banners that read **I AM RESPONSIBLE FOR MY DAY** and **I WANT RESPECT AND I SHOW IT** and hung them in school corridors. Daily messages on the themes of respect and responsibility are included in morning announcements and repeated on the electronic message board in the cafeteria.

The Middle Schools **S.M.I.L.E.** Club ("Students Motivated in Leading Each Other"), whose only qualification is that "you be a person who cares about others," raises funds for the school projects, sends a card to all students and staff members on their birthday, provides a buddy for new students to ease their school transition, and prepares and distributes to all students a monthly **Caring Calendar** with daily suggestions for how to show caring (e.g., "Compliment another student today," "Be kind to the office and cafeteria staff," "Compliment a teacher," "Don't spread rumors").

A **Positive Bus Program**, led by bus driver Mary Zimmerman, promotes respect and responsibility on all the school buses.

"There hasn't been a single parent complaint about the school teaching values," says Dee Serrio, President of Sweet Home's PTA Council. "Parents had input, and this whole program contains nothing more than the values parents said they wanted for their children."

Sweet Home's district wide values program has been written up in the New York Times, featured at the Annual Values Education Conference sponsored by the New York State Education Department, and presented at national conferences.

Contact: Sharon L. Banas, Values Education Coordinator, Sweet Home Middle School, 4150 Maple Road, Amherst, NY 14226; (716) 837-3500. Available for ordering: Sweet Home Values Education Handbook containing dozens of activities used in the program.

Source: **Center for the 4th & 5th Rs: Respect and Responsibility.** Online: http://www.cortland.edu/character/success/success06.htm.

Example 5 of Character Education Model
The Child Development Project

In the early 1980s, the Child Development Project (first piloted in San Ramon, California) set out to answer this question: Does a multifaceted character development program, begun in kindergarten and sustained throughout a child's elementary school years, make a measurable and lasting difference in a child's moral thinking, attitudes, and behavior? The CDP character program has five interlocking components:

1. A language arts curriculum that uses children's literature to reflect on values.
2. Cooperative learning, giving students regular practice in learning to work with others.
3. Discipline that uses class meetings to involve students in sharing responsibility for creating a classroom that respects others and supports learning.
4. School service programs, such as cross-age tutoring and "buddy classes" (e.g., a 5th grade class "adopts" a 2nd grade class), that enable older kids to help younger ones.
5. Family activities that offer parents ways to develop their children's character.

An example of component 5: Every two to three weeks, CDP teachers send home "family homework." "Family homework often consists of value-laden, sometimes humorous stories for families to read together and talk about. Other activities: "Discuss family chores" and "List 4 rules you must follow at home, then discuss with your parents the reason behind each rule."

Says a mother of a 3rd grade boy in a CDP school: "Once you get into it, it turns into fun. I learn things about Joey I never would have known. Instead of the usual, What did you do in school today?, conversations started by family homework let me discover the inside part of him."

In a longitudinal study, students in three CDP elementary schools, compared to students in matched control schools, were found to be: 1) more considerate and cooperative in their classrooms; 2) more likely to feel accepted by peers; 3) more skilled at solving interpersonal problems;

and 4) more strongly committed to democratic values such as including everyone in a decision.

In a follow-up study in eighth grade, students who had had the CDP program showed stronger conflict resolution skills, had greater self-esteem, were involved in more extracurricular activities, and were less likely to use marijuana or alcohol.

Developmental Studies CTR., 2000 Embarcadero, Suite 305, Oakland, CA 94606; (510) 533-0213.

Source: **Center for the 4th & 5th Rs: Respect and Responsibility.** Online: http://www.cortland.edu/character/success/success01.htm.

APPENDIX B

MAJOR STUDIES ON THE EFFECTIVENESS OF COMPUTERS AS LEARNING TOOLS

Study: Baker, E. L. Gearhart, M. and Herman, J.L. *Evaluation the Apple classrooms of tomorrow: Technology assessment in education and training.* Hillsdale, NJ: Lawrence Erlbaum Associates, 1994.

Participants: First through twelfth graders.

Design and Methods: Series of evaluation studies over a three-year period. Students and teachers were given Apple computers in the classroom and at home. Comparison groups in neighboring areas were chosen. Study conducted in five school sites located in California, Ohio, Minnesota, and Tennessee.

Findings:
- Apple Computers of Tomorrow (ACOT) had a positive impact on student attitudes.
- Overall, ACOT students did not perform better on standardized tests.

Study: Bangert-Drowns, R.L. The word processor as an instructional tool: A meta-analysis of word processing in writing instruction. *Review of Educational Research* (1993) 63:63-93.

Participants: Elementary school age through college age.

Design and Methods: Meta-analysis based on 32 comparative studies measuring post treatment performance criteria such as quality of writing, number of words, attitude toward writing, adherence to writing conventions, and frequency of revision.

Findings:
- Small effect on improvement of writing skills.
- Studies that focused on word processing the context of remedial writing yielded a larger effect.

Study: Clements, D.H. Enhancement of creativity in computer environments. *American Educational Research Journal* (1991) 28: 173-87.

Participants: 73 third graders-(mean age 8 years, 8 months).

Design and Methods: Pretest, posttest design over a 25 week period. Children matched on creativity and achievement were assigned to (1) Logo software, (2) non-computer creativity training, or (3) control. Study took place in New York.

Findings:
- Children who worked with Logo had increased figural (nonverbal) creativity.
- Both Logo and non-computer activities increased children's verbal creativity.

Study: Elliot, A., and Hall, N. The impact of self-regulatory teaching strategies on "at-risk" preschoolers' mathematical learning in a computer mediated environment. *Journal of Computing in Childhood Education* (1997) 8:187-98.

Participants: 54 pre-kindergarten students who were identified as at risk of early learning difficulties.

Design and Methods: Children were placed into three groups. Two used computer-based math activities and the third participated in non computer-based math activities (and used computers for other areas). Study took place in Australia.

Findings:
- Students in both groups that used computer-based activities scored significantly higher on the Test of Early Mathematical Ability—TEMA 2.

Study: Fletcher, J.D., Hawley, D.E., and Piele, P.K. Costs, effects and utility of microcomputer-assisted instruction in the classroom. Paper presented at the 7th International Conference on Technology and Education. Brussels, Belgium, 1999.

Participants: Third and fifth graders.

Design and Methods: Students at grade level received either computer-assisted instruction (CAI) or traditional math instruction for 71 days.

Findings: At both grade levels, students receiving CAI scored higher on a test of basic math skills than those who received traditional instruction only.

Study: Fletcher-Finn, C.M., and Gravatt, B. The efficacy of computer assisted instruction (CAI): A meta-analysis. *Journal of Educational Computing Research* (1995) 12:219-42.

Participants: Students from kindergarten through higher education.

Design and Methods: Meta-analysis of 120 studies conducted between 1987 and 1992. Looked at a range of factors including educational level, course content, publication year, duration of study, same or different teacher for the control group, and type of CAI.

Findings:
- No significant differences in study results for any of the factors.
- Gains in proficiency linked with only one factor: the quality of CAI materials.

Study: Foster, K., Erickson, G., Foster, D., et al. Computer-administered instruction in phonological awareness: Evaluation of the Daisy Quest program. Unpublished paper.

Participants: Pre-kindergarten and kindergarten children; 25 in first study; 70 in second study.

Design and Methods: Pretest, posttest design. Children randomly assigned to experimental group or control group. Experimental group received 16 to 20 sessions with DaisyQuest—a computerized program designed to increase phonological awareness.

Findings:
- In two different studies and five different measures of phonological awareness, the computer-based approach was found to be more effective than regular instruction.

Study: Gardner, C.M., Simmons, P.E., and Simpson, R.D. The effects of CAI and hands-on activities on elementary students' attitudes and weather knowledge. *School Science and Mathematics* (1992) 92:334-36.

Participants: Third graders.

Design and Methods: Comparative study of three groups in Georgia. First group received hands-on meteorology activities combined with software; second group received hands-on activities without software; and third group received traditional classroom instruction.

Findings:
- Children who had hands-on with software outperformed those who had hands-on without software.
- Both groups scored higher than those who had traditional instruction.

Study: Kulik, J.A. *Meta-analytic studies of findings on computer-based instruction. In Technology assessment in education and training.* Hillsdale, NJ: Lawrence Erlbaum Associates, 1994.

Participants: Students from kindergarten through higher education.

Design and Methods: Meta-analysis of more than 500 individual studies of computer-based instruction.

Findings:
- Students who used computer-based instruction scored higher on achievement tests, learned in less time, and were more likely to develop positive attitudes.

Study: Kulik, C. and Kulik, J.A. Effectiveness of computer-based instruction: An updated analysis. *Computers in Human Behavior* (1991) 7:75-94.

Participants: Students from kindergarten through higher education.

Design and Methods: Meta-analysis of 254 controlled-evaluation studies.

Findings:
- Computer-based instruction had a "moderate but significant" effect on achievement.

Study: Lazarowitz, R., and Huppert, J. Science process skills of 10th grade biology students in a computer-assisted learning setting. *Journal of Research on Computing in Education* (1993) 25:366-82.

Participants: High school students.

Design and Methods: Pretest, posttest design over four weeks in five biology classes in Israel. The experimental group received classroom laboratory instruction that included use of a software program. The control group received classroom instruction only.

Findings:
- Experimental group achieved higher mean score on the posttest.
- No significant difference between the groups by gender.

Study: Mann, D., Shakesshaft, C., Becker, J., et al. *West Virginia's Basic Skills/Computer Education program: An analysis of achievement.* Santa Monica., CA: Millken Family Foundation, 1999.

Participants: Representative sample of 950 fifth grade students from 18 elementary schools.

Design and Methods: Study of students who used Basic Skills/Computer Education program in West Virginia. Several variables were analyzed including intensity of use, prior achievement sociodemography, teacher training, and teacher and student attitudes.

Findings:
- The more students participated in the program, the more their test scores improved.
- Consistent access, positive attitudes toward the equipment, and teacher training in the technology led to the greatest achievement gains.

Study: Mayfield-Stewart, C., Morre, P., Sharp, D., et al. Evaluation of multimedia instruction on learning and transfer. Paper presented at the Annual Conference of the American Education Research. New Orleans, 1994.

Participants: At risk inner-city kindergartners.

Design and Methods: Children exposed to a multimedia environment (Multimedia Environments that Organize and Support Text) for language development for three months were compared with children in a conventional kindergarten classroom.

Findings:
- Study group showed superior gains in auditory skills and language skills, were able to tell stories better, and showed better

use of tense.

Study: Nastasi, B. K., Clements, D. H., and Battista, M.T. Social-cognitive interactions, motivation, and cognitive growth in Logo programming and CAI problem-solving environments. *Journal of Educational Psychology* (1990) 82:150-58.

Participants: 12 fourth graders and 28 sixth graders.

Design and Methods: Pretest, posttest design over 22 weeks. Pairs of students were randomly assigned to either Logo activities or CAI problem-solving programs to investigate whether children exhibited differing amounts of behaviors indicative of cooperative interaction, conflict resolution, effectance motivation, and self-evaluation.

Study: Nastasi, B. K. and Clements, D.H. Effectance motivation, perceived scholastic competence, and higher-order thinking in two cooperative computer environments. *Journal of Educational Psychology* (1994) 10:249-75.

Participants: 48 third graders working in pairs.

Design and Methods: Pretest, posttest design. Participants randomly assigned to either Logo or curriculum-based instruction in writing to examine whether qualitatively distinct computer environments engender social experiences that enhance motivation for learning.

Findings:
- Results suggest that evaluation of success was internally determined in the Logo environment, though students still sought external approval.
- Logo enhanced effectance motivation and higher-order thinking.

Study: Raghavan, K. Sartoris, M.L. and Glaser, R. The impact of model-centered instruction on student learning: The area and volume units. *Journal of Computers in Mathematics and Science Teaching* (1997) 16:363-404.

Participants: 110 sixth graders (50 boys and 60 girls).

Design and Methods: Eight-week curriculum to teach in Pennsylvania concepts of area and volume using a computer-based program in addition to traditional instruction. At the end of the course, students were tested and their scores compared with eighth graders who had received traditional instruction only.

Findings:
- Computer-based program increased students' reasoning skills.
- The sixth-grade students scored better overall than the eighth-grade students, especially on more complex problems.

Study: Ryan, A. W. Meta-analysis of achievement effects of microcomputer applications in elementary schools. *Educational Administration Quarterly* (1991) 27:161-84.

Participants: Elementary school-children (grades K-6); each study with a sample size of at least 40.

Design and Methods: Meta-analysis of comparative studies. Variables analyzed included characteristics of students, teachers, physical settings, and instructional formats.

Findings:
- Amount of technology-related teacher training significantly related to achievement of students.

Study: Scardamalia, M. Bereiter, C., McLean, R., et al. Computer-supported intentional learning environments. *Journal of Educational Computing Research* (1989) 5:51-68.

Participants: Fifth and sixth graders.

Design and Methods: Students worked with a collaborative computer application. Computer Supported International Learning Environment (CSILE), daily for almost eight months.

Findings:
- Independent thinking student reflection, and progressive thought were maximized by CSILE.

Study: Schultz, L.H. Pilot validation study of the Scholastic Beginning Literacy System (Wiggle Works) 1994-95 midyear report. Unpublished paper. February 1995.

Participants: First graders.

Design and Methods: Three-month study in two suburban systems

(California and Massachusetts) and one urban- system (Massachusetts), in which the study group used interactive storybooks in addition to traditional instruction to support reading, writing, speaking and listening; control group received traditional instruction only.

Findings: Study group demonstrated an increase in basic language skills.

Study: Stone, T.T. III. The academic impact of classroom computer usage upon middle-class primary grade level elementary school children. Ph.D. dissertation, 1996. Abstract in *Dissertation Abstracts International:* 57/06-A.

Participants: 114 second graders.

Design and Methods: Students the same age, same socioeconomic status, and using the same curriculum were compared across two schools in the same district. One group used computer-assisted instruction (CAI), one did not.

Findings: Children who used CAI since kindergarten achieved a significant improvement in vocabulary, reading, spelling, and math problem solving achievement.

Study: Wenglinksy, H. *Does it compute? The relationship between educational technology and student achievement in mathematics.* Princeton, NJ: Educational Testing Service, 1998.

Participation: Fourth and eighth graders.

Design and Methods: National assessment of the effects of simulation and higher-order thinking technologies on math achievement. Data analyzed controlling for socioeconomic status, class size and teacher characteristics.

Findings:
- Students who used the software showed gains in math level.
- Students whose teachers received training showed gains in math scores.

Source: Roschelle, Jeremy M., Roy D. Pea, Christopher M. Hoadley, Douglas N. Gordin and Barbara M. Means. Changing how and what children learn in school with computer-based technologies. *The Future of Children*, 10:76-101. Website: www.futureofchildren.org.